Table of Contents

Introduction

The Stories

Types of Stories
- fairy tales
- fables
- realistic fiction
- nonfiction
- poetry

Ways to Use the Stories

1. Directed lessons
   - with small groups of students reading at the same level
   - with an individual student

2. Partner reading

3. With cooperative learning groups
   - at school
   - at home

Things to Consider

1. Determine your purpose for selecting a story—instructional device, partner reading, group work, or independent reading. Each purpose calls for a different degree of story difficulty.

2. A single story may be used for more than one purpose. You might first use the story as an instructional tool, have partners read the story a second time for greater fluency, and then use the story at a later time for independent reading.

3. When presenting a story to a group or an individual for the first time, review any vocabulary that will be difficult to decode or understand. Many students will benefit from a review of the vocabulary page and the questions before they read the story.

Types of Skill Pages

Five pages of activities covering a variety of reading skills follow each story:

- comprehension
- vocabulary
- phonics
- structural analysis
- parts of speech
- record information

Ways to Use the Skill Pages

1. Individualize skill practice for each student with tasks that are appropriate for his or her needs.

2. As directed minilessons, the skill pages may be used in several ways:

   - Make a transparency for students to follow as you work through the lesson.

   - Write the activity on the board and call on students to fill in the answers.

   - Reproduce the page for everyone to use as you direct the lesson.

3. When using the skill pages for independent practice, make sure that the skills have been introduced to the reader. Review the directions and check for understanding. Review the completed lesson with the student to determine if further practice is needed.

Stan and Goldie

Alex was looking for his cat. The cat didn't come when Alex called his name. He didn't come when Alex shook his food box. That was bad news. When Stan didn't come for food, he was up to no good.

Alex was right. Stan was about to do something bad. He was sitting on the table watching Goldie swim in her bowl. Around and around went Goldie. Around and around went Stan's eyes. The naughty cat slowly put a paw into the bowl. Just as he was about to grab Goldie, Alex saw him.

"Scat, cat!" yelled Alex. "Yow!" screeched Stan. He took off like a flash and hid under the sofa.

Now Goldie lives in a new home with a wire lid across the top. And Stan has to be happy with fish out of a can.

Questions about *Stan and Goldie*

1. What kinds of pets did Alex have?

_____

2. How did Alex try to get Stan to come to him?

_____

3. Why didn't Stan come when Alex called him?

_____

4. What did Alex do to protect Goldie?

_____

5. What would have happened if Alex had not found Stan?

_____

6. What do you think will happen to Stan if he tries to catch Goldie again?

_____

Think about It

Think of another way to protect the fish from Stan. Draw a picture to show what you would do.

Name _____

What Happened Next?

Cut out the sentences below.
Paste them in order.

1.

2.

3.

4.

5.

6.

✂ -

Stan was sitting on the table watching Goldie.

Stan didn't come when Alex shook his food box.

"Scat, cat!" yelled Alex.

Goldie lives in a home with a wire lid across the top.

Stan took off like a flash and hid under the sofa.

Stan put a paw into the bowl of water.

Name _____

Match the Parts

Match:

1. naughty   a cover for a box or a dish

2. bowl   an animal's foot

3. wire   to take hold of suddenly

4. paw   a thin piece of metal

5. grab   not behaving well

6. lid   a kind of deep dish

Circle the answer.

1. It was **bad news**.
   a. a funny story
   b. not a good thing
   c. an old newspaper

2. He was **up to no good**.
   a. going to do something bad
   b. climbing a tree
   c. standing on his hind legs

3. Stan took off **like a flash**.
   a. with a flashlight
   b. to light a firecracker
   c. running very fast

Name _____

The Letter X

Write the letter **x** on each line. Read the words.

Ale____   fo____   Ma____   ne____t

bo____   e____it   mi____er   fi____

Fill in the missing words.

1. _____ and _____ went to a ball game.

2. Mom used a _____ to make pancakes.

3. The little _____ ran into its den.

4. Go out the door marked _____.

5. Put that fork _____ to the plate.

6. What is in that big _____?

7. Will you help me _____ my broken toy?

What Rhymes?

Write words that rhyme with these words.

1. scat _____   _____   _____

2. do _____   _____   _____

3. paw _____   _____   _____

4. bad _____   _____   _____

Name _____

Stan and Goldie

1. Draw a fish in the bowl. Color it orange.
2. Draw blue water and a green plant in the bowl.
3. Draw a big, black-and-white cat looking at the bowl.
   Make one cat paw going into the bowl.
4. Write the cat's name under the cat.
5. Write the fish's name over the bowl.

Boots

"Emma, look at this lettuce. Something is eating up my garden," said Tony. "I planted this lettuce for us to eat. I'm going to catch that hungry little pest."

Tony got a box and poked some holes in it. He took the box, a stick, and some string to the garden. Tony set his trap right over a big, green lettuce plant. He set one side of the box on the stick. He tied one end of the string to the stick. Then he hid behind a big plant. Tony held on to the string. He sat and waited a long time.

At last Tony saw the lettuce leaves begin to wiggle. Soon a little pink nose and two eyes peeked out of the green leaves. Tony pulled the string and down came the box. The lettuce eater was caught!

Tony reached under the box and lifted out the little pest. "Emma, come see what I have," he called.

When Emma got to the garden, she saw a furry rabbit. It was black with little white feet. "Let's call her Boots," said Emma. "I think she will make a good pet."

"I'll build you a big pen in the backyard," Tony told Boots.

Boots did make a good pet. When Tony called "Boots!" she came hopping to them. She stood on her back legs to take treats from Emma's hand. She used the cat's litter box when she came in the house. And she never went into the garden to eat Tony's lettuce again!

Name _____

Questions about *Boots*

1. How did Tony know there was a pest in his garden?

   _____

2. What did Tony use to trap the rabbit?

   _____

3. How did Tony know when to pull the string on the trap?

   _____

4. Where did Tony build the pen for Boots?

   _____

5. Circle the things Boots could do.

   come when her name was called   use the cat's litter box

   climb a tree   open a can of food

   take treats from someone's hand   catch mice and bugs

   make loud noises   stand on her back legs

6. Why did Emma name the rabbit "Boots"?

   _____

Think about It

Pretend you have a pest in your garden.
Think of a way to capture the pest.
On another paper, draw a picture to show what you would do.

What Happened Next?

Cut out the sentences below.
Paste them in order.

1.

2.

3.

4.

5.

6.

✂

Tony reached under the box and lifted out the little pest.

Boots never went into the garden to eat Tony's lettuce again.

"Something is eating up my garden," said Tony.

Tony set his trap over a big, green lettuce plant.

Boots was a good pet. She came when Tony called her name.

When Emma got to the garden she saw a furry rabbit.

Name _____

What Does It Mean?

Circle the answer.

1. In this story **Boots** means
    a. a name for a pet
    b. something to wear on your feet

2. In this story **pet** means
    a. to rub gently
    b. an animal kept as a friend

3. In this story **treat** means
    a. to give medicine to a sick person
    b. a snack

4. In this story **plant** means
    a. something growing in the garden
    b. a factory

Opposites

Write the opposites of these words.

1. she _____   6. sick _____

2. in _____   7. back _____

3. came _____   8. come _____

4. good _____   9. little _____

5. hungry _____   10. tie _____

Word Box				
out	he	big	full	go
went	bad	untie	front	well

Name _____

The Sound of K

All of these words have the sound **k**.
A different letter or letters make the sound in each word.

come   sti**ck**   **k**ite

Write the letters that make the sound **k** in these words.

1. back   _ck_   6. look   _____

2. hike   _____   7. came   _____

3. called   _____   8. duck   _____

4. coat   _____   9. kitten   _____

5. block   _____   10. kick   _____

Who Owns It?

Add **'s** to these names.
Draw a line to what they own.

Tony_____ lettuce

Emma_____ apron

Ruff_____ bone

rabbit_____ carrot

Ramon_____ mitt

Lee_____ wagon

Name _____

Tony

Write about a time in the story when Tony felt this way.

2. Tony was angry when _____

_____.

2. Tony was smart when _____

_____.

3. Tony was surprised when _____

_____.

4. Tony was kind when _____

_____.

5. Tony was happy when _____.

Little Red Hen

Little Red Hen lived on a small farm with a duck, a cat, and a dog. Little Red Hen was busy all the time. But the duck only wanted to swim in the pond. The cat only wanted to nap in a sunny spot. The dog only wanted to run and play.

One day Little Red Hen found some wheat seeds. "Who will help me plant these seeds?" she asked.

"I won't," quacked the wee brown duck. "It's time to go to the pond."

"I won't," purred the small yellow cat. "It's time to take a nap."

"I won't," growled the big black dog. "It's time to chase my tail."

"Then I'll do it myself," said Little Red Hen. And she did.

The wheat grew tall and yellow. It was time to harvest the wheat. "Who will help me cut the wheat?" asked Little Red Hen.

"I won't," quacked the wee brown duck. "It's time to eat my lunch."

"I won't," purred the small yellow cat. "It's time to climb a tree."

"I won't," growled the big black dog. "It's time to fetch a stick."

"Then I'll do it myself," said Little Red Hen. And she did.

The wheat was ready to grind into flour. "Who will help me take the wheat to the mill?" she asked.

"I won't," quacked the wee brown duck. "It's time to rest in the sun."

"I won't," purred the small yellow cat. "It's time to chase a bird."

"I won't," growled the big black dog. "It's time to scratch my fleas."

"Then I'll do it myself," said Little Red Hen. And she did.

The wheat was made into flour at the mill. "Who will help me make the flour into bread?" she asked.

"I won't," quacked the wee brown duck. "It's time to eat green weeds."

"I won't," purred the small yellow cat. "It's time to clean my fur."

"I won't," growled the big black dog. "It's time to dig a hole."

"Then I'll do it myself," said Little Red Hen. And she did.

Little Red Hen took the hot brown bread out of the oven. It smelled so good! "Who will help me eat this bread?" she asked.

"We will!" shouted the wee brown duck, the small yellow cat, and the big black dog. "It's time to have a snack!"

"Oh, no, you won't!" said Little Red Hen. "You didn't help plant the seeds. You didn't help cut the wheat. You did not help take it to the mill. You didn't help bake the bread. Now you cannot eat the bread."

"Here chick, chick, chick," she called. Little Red Hen and her chicks ate up all the bread.

Name _____

Questions about *Little Red Hen*

1. Who lived on the small farm?

   _____

2. Tell four things Little Red Hen did after she found the seeds.

   _____   _____

   _____   _____

3. What did the duck, cat, and dog say when Little Red Hen asked them to help?

   _____

4. Why didn't Little Red Hen let the duck, cat, and dog eat the bread?

   _____

   _____

5. Find three words in the story that mean **not big**.

   _____   _____   _____

6. Why do you think the animals would not help Little Red Hen?

   _____

7. Do you think the animals will help next time? Why?

   _____

Number the pictures in order to tell the story.

Name _____

What Does It Mean?

Write the word by its meaning.
You will not use all the words.

mill   harvest   grind
nap   fetch   flour
flea   oven   scratch

1. the place bread is baked   _____

2. to go and get something   _____

3. a short sleep   _____

4. a small insect that feeds on animal blood   _____

5. a place where grain is ground into flour   _____

6. to gather ripe crops   _____

Real or Make-Believe?

Make an **X** if a real hen can do it.
Make a ✓ if a real hen cannot do it.

_____ A hen can talk.

_____ A hen can eat seeds and bugs.

_____ A hen can bake bread.

_____ A hen can plant seeds.

_____ A hen can live on a farm.

_____ A hen can run.

Missing Sounds

Write the missing sounds in these words.

br   tr   gr

_____asshopper   _____ead   _____ee

_____oom   _____ain   _____apes

Contractions

Write the contractions for these words.

1. did not _____   4. will not _____

2. I will _____   5. cannot _____

3. it is _____   6. I am _____

Word Box		
I'll	I'm	it's
won't	can't	didn't

Name _____

What Does It Look Like?

Circle the words that describe.

wee	chick	brown	farm
sunny	tall	small	run
yellow	hot	little	black
red	big	seed	pond

Write the words that describe.

_____ _____ dog

_____ _____ hen

_____ _____ cat

_____ _____ duck

_____ _____ bread

Who Said It?

1. "It's time to go to the pond," said the _____.

2. "It's time to fetch a stick," said the _____.

3. "It's time to climb a tree," said the _____.

4. "Here chick, chick, chick," called the _____.

Are You a Spider?

Pat, Pam, and Pete are triplets. They like creepy, crawly things like bugs and worms. Today they are searching for a spider.

"Let's go find a spider," said Pat. "We can look in the backyard. I think we can find a spider there."

"But we don't know what a spider looks like," said Pam. "How big is it? What color is it? How will we know when we find one?"

The triplets searched all over the backyard. Pat found something on a bush. "Are you a spider?" she asked.

"No. I'm a grasshopper. I am an insect. I have six legs. A spider has eight legs," answered a big brown grasshopper.

Pam found something under a pile of leaves. "Are you a spider?" she asked.

"No. I'm an ant. I am an insect. My body has three parts. A spider has two parts," answered the tiny red ant.

Pete found something on a rose plant. "Are you a spider?" he asked.

"No. I'm a butterfly. I am an insect. I have wings. A spider doesn't have wings," answered the pretty orange butterfly.

The triplets met on the back porch. "Did you find a spider?" Pete asked his sisters.

"No, we didn't. But we know a spider has eight legs and two body parts," said Pam. "Did you find one?"

"No, but I know a spider doesn't have wings," said Pete. Just then Pete saw something. "Look up there!" Pam and Pat looked up. In the corner of the porch roof was a big web. Hanging down from the web was a shiny black body. It had eight legs and two body parts. It did not have wings.

"It's a spider!" shouted Pat with a grin. "I knew we would find a spider."

Name _____

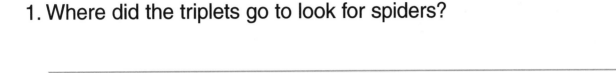

Questions about *Are You a Spider?*

1. Where did the triplets go to look for spiders?

   _____

2. What did they find?

   Pat _____   Pam _____

   Pete _____

3. Where did the triplets find the spider?

   _____

4. How did they know it was a spider?

   _____

5. What kind of an animal is a grasshopper, an ant, and
   a butterfly?

   _____

6. What part of this story is make-believe?

   _____

What gets caught in the spider's web? Circle the answer.

What Happened Next?

Cut out the sentences below.
Paste them in order.

"Let's go find a spider," said Pat.

1.

2.

3.

4.

5.

6.

"I knew we would find a spider," said Pat with a grin.

- ✂ - - -

Pete said, "Look up there."

Pat saw a big brown grasshopper.

A spider was hanging from a big web.

The triplets went into the backyard.

Pete saw a pretty orange butterfly.

Pam saw a tiny red ant.

Name _____

What Does It Mean?

Write the word by its meaning.

triplets   web   spider
creepy   porch   grin

1. a smile   _____

2. three children born at the same
   time to the same mother   _____

3. a silk trap spun by a spider   _____

4. a covered entrance to a building   _____

5. scary or spooky   _____

6. a small animal with eight legs   _____

What Does It Look Like?

Circle the words that describe something.
Use the words to fill in the blanks.

brown   red   tiny   shiny
orange   black   big   pretty

1. a _____ _____ grasshopper

2. a _____ _____ butterfly

3. a _____ _____ ant

4. a _____ _____ spider

Name _____

Silent *K*

When you read **kn**, the **k** does not make a sound. You say just the sound of **n**.

know   **kn**ot   **kn**ew   **kn**ock

Write **kn** on each line. Read the word you make. Draw a picture of the word.

door____ob	____ee	____ife

Words That Sound the Same

Read the words to a friend.

heard   herd   eight   ate
ant   aunt   knew   new

Fill in the missing words.

1. My _____ came for a visit.

2. We _____ pizza for lunch.

3. Raul _____ a loud noise.

4. Are those _____ shoes?

5. He _____ how to play the game.

6. A spider has _____ legs.

Name _____

Spiders and Insects

Make an **X** in the box.

	spider	insect
8 legs		
6 legs		
3 body parts		
2 body parts		
no wings		
wings		

Color the spiders.
Make an **X** on the insects.

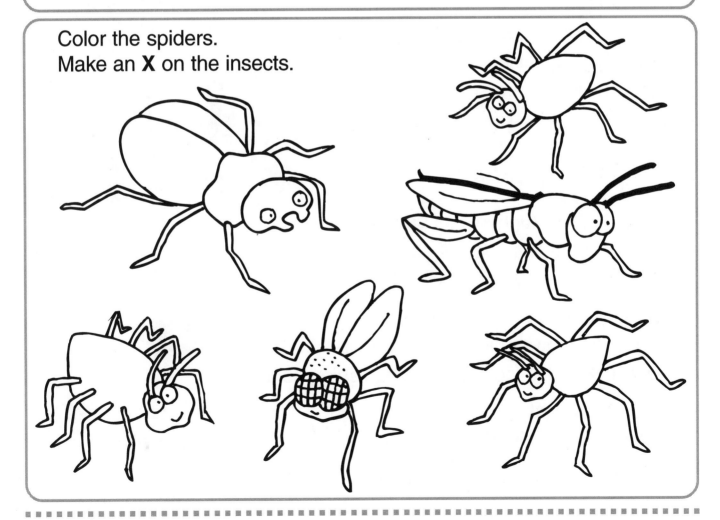

Ice Fishing with Grandfather

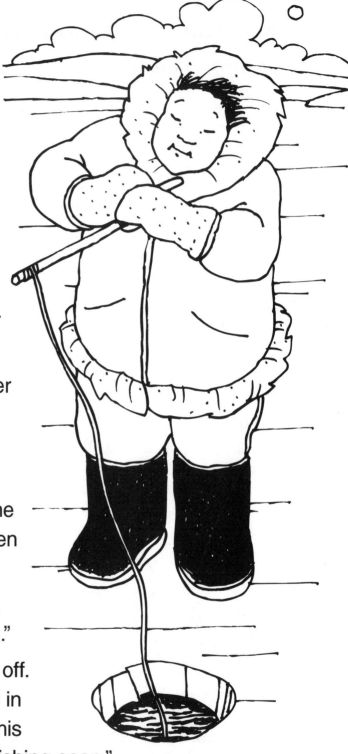

Will sat at his desk. He looked at his teacher, but he did not hear her. His mind was far away. "Grandfather will be here soon," he thought.

When school was out, Will ran home. He didn't stop at the store. He didn't stop at his friend's house. He didn't stop until he saw his father. "Is Grandfather here yet?" he asked.

"Be patient, Will. Your grandfather will be here soon," answered Father.

Will ran into the house. His mother was busy cooking. She laughed when she saw Will. "Be patient, Will. Your grandfather will be here soon."

Just then someone walked into the kitchen. "Grandfather, you're here! When can we go?" shouted Will.

Grandfather laughed. "Be patient, Will. We must eat first. We will go soon."

At last Will and Grandfather were off. They raced across the flat, frozen land in Grandfather's snowmobile. Will pulled his parka up around his face. "We will be fishing soon."

Will stood next to Grandfather. He put his fishing line into the hole. He jiggled the line. Grandfather laughed. "Be patient, Will. We will be eating fish soon."

Name _____

Questions about *Ice Fishing with Grandfather*

1. What did Will do when school was over?

_____

2. Why was Will in a hurry to get home?

_____

3. Where were Will and his grandfather going?

_____

4. What was his mother doing when Will got home?

_____

5. Why did Grandfather and Will use a snowmobile to go fishing?

_____

6. Why didn't Will hear his teacher that afternoon?

_____

Write the words for each picture.

_____   _____

Name _____

What Happened Next?

Number the sentences in order.

_____ Will ran home.

_____ Will fished in a hole in the ice.

_____ Will spoke to his father.

_____ Will rode on a snowmobile with his grandfather.

_____ Will did not hear his teacher.

_____ Will's mother was cooking.

Draw what you think happened next.

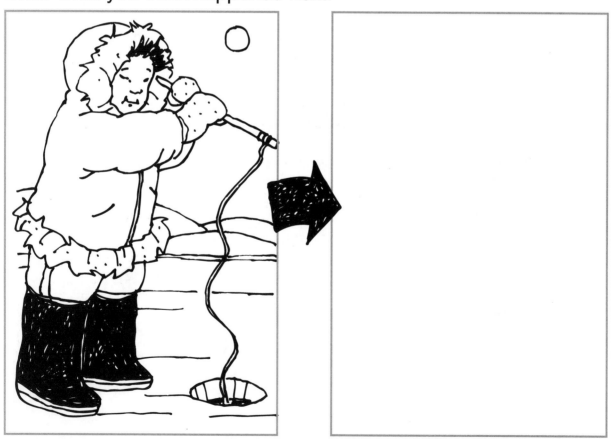

Name _____

What Does It Mean?

Match:

1. teacher	in a short time from now
2. soon	to make happy sounds
3. kitchen	to become hard or solid because of cold
4. laugh	a person who helps you learn
5. frozen	a room where food is cooked

Color the circle to tell what the words mean.

1. His mind was far away.
   - ○ He was on a trip.
   - ○ He was thinking of something else.
   - ○ He was asleep.

2. Be patient!
   - ○ You need to go to the doctor.
   - ○ Do what you are told.
   - ○ Don't be in such a hurry.

Compound Words

Use these words to make compound words.

grand	snow	fly	ball
butter	cow	father	corn
mobile	pop	base	boy

1. _____   4. _____

2. _____   5. _____

3. _____   6. _____

Name _____

Vowels

Circle the words that have these short vowels.

a—am   **e**—Ed   **i**—it   **o**—off   **u**—up

Will	sat	desk	his	fun
soon	mind	yet	far	ran
must	eat	on	stop	hear

The Sounds of *ed*

Write each word under the letter or letters that make the sound you hear at the end of the word.

ed	d	t
_____	_____	_____
_____	_____	_____
_____	_____	_____
_____	_____	_____
_____	_____	_____

filled	walked	painted
wanted	pulled	laughed
looked	raced	named
shouted	jiggled	lifted
played	wished	planted

Name _____

Words That Sound the Same

Read the words to a friend.

hear	here	beet	beat	red	read
blue	blew	son	sun	by	buy

Fill in the missing words.

1. "Did you _____ that noise?" shouted Jamal.

2. Mr. Mason took his _____ to a ball game.

3. I _____ *Frog and Toad Are Friends* for a
   book report.

4. "Will you _____ some of my cookies?" asked the
   girl scout.

5. Don't _____ that drum in the house.

6. The wind _____ my kite into the tree.

Pronouns

Write a pronoun for each noun.

it   he   she   they   we

1. parka _____   5. you and I _____

2. mother _____   6. snowmobile _____

3. Will _____   7. grandfather _____

4. friends _____   8. kitchen _____

Eric and the Bathtub

My little brother Eric is two years old. He loves everybody and everything. But what he likes best is the bathtub. Eric doesn't care if the bathtub is full or empty.

When Mom gives him a bath, she has to pull him screaming out of the tub. "Eric, you've been in the tub for half an hour. It's time to put on your pajamas and go to bed."

"No, no," screams Eric. "No jammies. Stay here."

If the tub is empty, Eric throws his toys over the side into the tub. Then he climbs in. He plays until we make him get out. We have to keep the door shut to keep him out of the tub.

Yesterday Eric gave me a big scare. I filled the tub with bubble bath and water. Before I got into the tub, the telephone rang. I shut the bathroom door and went to pick up the phone. A minute later, when I came back, the bathroom door was open. Eric was in the tub with all his clothes on. He was covered with bubbles. And he wasn't alone. There in the tub with Eric was our dog Pete.

"Eric, what are you doing?" I yelled.

"I'm givin' Pete a baf, Sarah," he said.

I yanked Eric and Pete out of the tub and called my mother. Mother dried them off. Then she asked, "How did you get in the bathroom?"

Eric reached up and turned the doorknob. "I'm a big boy," he said with a happy smile.

Last night Dad put a lock on the bathroom door. He put the key where Eric can't reach it.

More Read and Understand • Grade 2 • EMC 746

Name _____

Questions about *Eric and the Bathtub*

1. What does Eric like best?

_____

2. What does Eric do when his mother takes him out of the bathtub?

_____

3. Why did they have to keep the bathroom door shut?

_____

4. How did Eric get into the bathroom?

_____

5. What did Eric's father do to keep Eric out of the bathroom?

_____

6. Why was the sister scared when she saw Eric and Pete in the bathtub?

_____

Draw the picture for each word.

doorknob	bubbles
bathtub	key

Name _____

What Happened Next?

Number the pictures in order.

Name _____

What Does It Mean?

Write the word by its meaning.

1. clothes to wear in bed   _____

2. a boy who has the same parents
   as another person   _____

3. has nothing in it   _____

4. a way to keep something closed   _____

5. to make a loud noise   _____

6. a tool used to lock a door   _____

7. another word for pulled   _____

8. all by yourself   _____

brother	alone	empty	lock
pajamas	yanked	key	scream

Eric cannot say some words yet.
What did he mean when he said these words?

1. jammies _____

2. baf _____

Name _____

Silent E

An **e** at the end of a word can make the vowel sound long.

can + **e** = cane   pin + **e** = pine

Circle the missing words.

1. I took a bath in the _____.   tub   tube

2. Eric has a little _____ of milk left.   bit   bite

3. Connie ate a red and green candy _____.   can   cane

4. Hand me that _____ of toothpaste.   tub   tube

5. Can I have a _____ of your cake?   bit   bite

6. What kind of soup is in that _____?   can   cane

Opposites

Write the opposites of these words.

1. full _____   5. big _____

2. open _____   6. tell _____

3. girl _____   7. out _____

4. here _____   8. under _____

Word Box			
over	in	empty	shut
boy	little	there	ask

Name _____

Bathtub—Shower

How are a bathtub and a shower alike?

_____

_____

How are a bathtub and a shower different?

_____

_____

I like to take a _____ best.

                    bath   shower

Masumi's Party

Masumi invited five friends to a party. It was her birthday, and she wanted a picnic at the park. Her friends came at noon. Balloons and funny hats were on the picnic table. Small sacks were sitting by the plates. "Find the sack with your name," said Masumi. "That's your place to sit."

Masumi's friends found their places and sat down. Soon everyone had on a funny hat. "What's in the sack?" asked Lena.

"You will see later," answered Masumi. Mother made sushi and pink lemonade for the party. That was what Masumi wanted. There were hot dogs and potato chips, too.

After lunch everyone played in the park. They slid down the slide and swung on the swings. They took turns going on the teeter-totter.

"It's time for birthday cake," called Mother. Everyone ran back to the picnic table. Masumi made a wish and blew out her candles. After cake and presents she said, "Now you can open your sacks." Everyone found something they liked in the sack.

"Thank you, Masumi," said all her friends.

Soon it was time to go home. A happy crowd of friends walked out of the park. They all had funny hats, balloons, and a nice surprise from Masumi.

Masumi hugged her mother and whispered, "This was the best party I ever had. Thank you, Mother."

Questions about *Masumi's Party*

1. What kind of party did Masumi have?

   _____

2. Who came to the party?

   _____

3. How was the table set?

   _____

4. What did they eat for lunch?

   _____

5. What did Masumi and her friends play on at the park?

   _____

6. When did the children get to look in the sacks?

   _____

7. How did Masumi feel about her party?

   _____

A Birthday Party

Get a sheet of paper. Write about a birthday party.
Be sure to answer these questions.

   Where was the party?
   What did you eat?
   What did you do?

Name _____

What Happened Next?

Cut out the sentences below.
Paste them in order.

Masumi invited five friends to a picnic.

1.

2.

3.

4.

5.

6.

"This was the best party I ever had," Masumi told her mother.

✂ --

They ate sushi and drank pink lemonade. There were hot dogs and potato chips, too.

Masumi's friends came to Green Park.

They had birthday cake and Masumi opened her presents.

They played on the swings, slide, and teeter-totter.

Masumi's friends opened the sacks. "Thank you, Masumi," they said.

Everyone went home with a balloon, a funny hat, and a surprise in a sack.

Name _____

What Does It Mean?

Use these words to answer the riddles. You will not use all of the words.

sack	lunch	picnic	teeter-totter
hat	balloon	swing	lemonade
slide	friend	sushi	park

You sit on this and go up and down. _____	You can carry things in this. _____	This is someone who likes you, too. _____
This is an outdoor meal. _____	This is a rubber toy filled with air. _____	You wear this on your head. _____
This is a meal you eat at noon. _____	This is a food made from rice and fish. _____	This is something to drink. _____

Name _____

Long A

Read the words.
Circle the words with the sound of long **a**.

place	name	back	table
came	hats	plate	said
park	drank	Saturday	glad
sack	stay	after	played

Do—Did

Write the words in the boxes.

drink	drank	swing	eat
slid	ate	saw	swung
see	sit	slide	sat

I do it.	I did it.
_____	_____
_____	_____
_____	_____
_____	_____
_____	_____

Name _____

What Is in the Sack?

Look at the picture. Read what Masumi is saying.
Color in the circle to answer the question.

What is in the sacks?
- ○ lunch
- ○ surprises for her friends
- ○ nothing

I hope you like what is in your sack.

What is in Lena's sack?
- ○ pencils
- ○ a brush and paints
- ○ green and blue paper

Will you paint me a picture, Lena?

What is in Kelly's sack?
- ○ jacks and a ball
- ○ a little bear
- ○ candy hearts

Can I play with your game, Kelly?

What is in Tonya's sack?
- ○ blue socks
- ○ a little purse
- ○ a red ribbon

That will look pretty in your hair, Tonya.

What is in Sally's sack?
- ○ a book
- ○ paper dolls
- ○ a diary

I hope you like this story, Sally.

It's Snowing!

Snow is falling to the ground
Leaving lacy flakes around.

A snowy day is a lot of fun! Put on your mittens and boots and run outside. Make snow angels or a big snowman. Or jump on your sled and race down a hill. But where does all that snow come from?

Clouds are made of tiny drops of water. When these drops of water freeze, snowflakes are made. The snowflakes get bigger and heavier. Then they fall to earth.

If the land is warm, the snowflakes melt when they hit the ground. If the land is cold, the snow stays. Soon the ground is covered with a blanket of white. Trees, bushes, and rooftops wear white coats, too.

Snowflakes have six sides. Most of them are flat. No two snowflakes look just alike. The next time it snows, catch a snowflake on a piece of black paper. Look at the snowflake before it melts. Can you count the six sides? Can you find two that are just alike?

48

Name _____

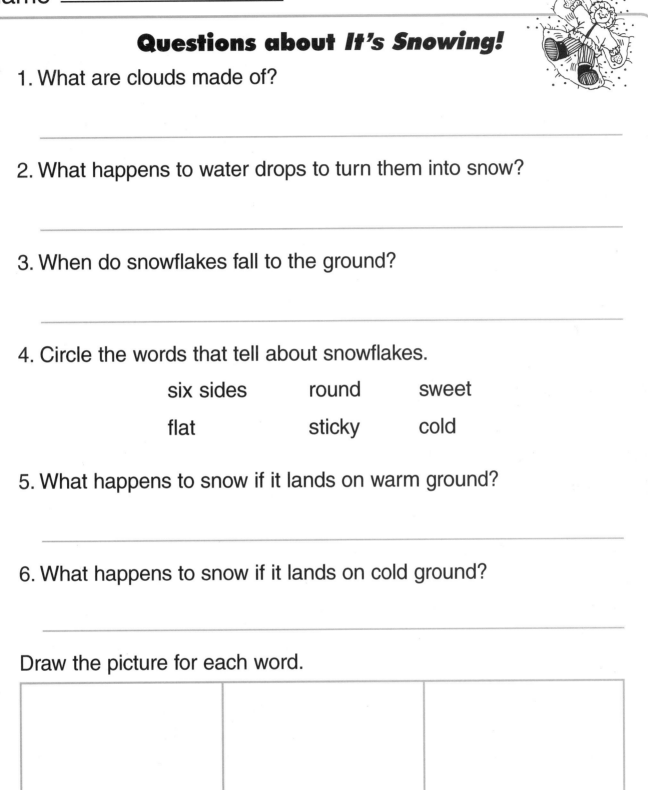

Questions about *It's Snowing!*

1. What are clouds made of?

   _____

2. What happens to water drops to turn them into snow?

   _____

3. When do snowflakes fall to the ground?

   _____

4. Circle the words that tell about snowflakes.

six sides	round	sweet
flat	sticky	cold

5. What happens to snow if it lands on warm ground?

   _____

6. What happens to snow if it lands on cold ground?

   _____

Draw the picture for each word.

snowman	snow angel	mittens and boots

Name _____

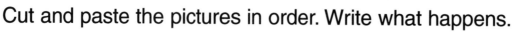

What Happened Next?

Cut and paste the pictures in order. Write what happens.

paste	paste
_____ _____	_____ _____
paste	paste
_____ _____ _____	_____ _____ _____

     More Read and Understand • Grade 2 • EMC 746

Name _____

What Does It Mean?

Write the word by its meaning.

1. frozen flakes falling from the sky   _____

2. to make water solid   _____

3. a group of water drops in the sky   _____

4. looks like lace   _____

5. to turn from ice to water   _____

6. to go fast   _____

7. used to ride on snow   _____

8. the same   _____

snow	race	lacy	freeze
cloud	alike	sled	melt

Two Sounds of *ow*

Read the words. Write the sound you hear.

d**ow**n–**ow**   sn**ow**–**ō**

1. grow   _ō_   5. mower _____   9. low _____

2. wow _____   6. crowd _____   10. now _____

3. flower _____   7. show _____

4. blow _____   8. frown _____

Name _____

Two Ways to Spell the Same Sound

The **ow** in cr**ow**d has the same sound as the **ou** in ar**ou**nd.
Use **ow** or **ou** to complete the words below.

cl____d   cl____n   m____se

c____   fl____er   h____se

Er—Or

Underline the letters that make the sound **er** as in h**er.**

water   worm   fern

butter   dancer   color

flavor   flower   doctor

Write sentences using two of the words. Underline the **er** words.

1. _____

2. _____

Name _____

Make a Snowflake

1. Cut out the square.
2. Fold it like this:

a.

b.

c.

3. Cut.

a.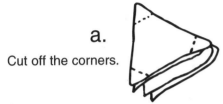

Cut off the corners.

b.

Make cuts in the sides.

4. Open the snowflake.

Stickers

Candy ran through the weeds in the vacant lot. Morris chased after his dog. "Come here, Candy," he called. Candy ran back and sat down in front of Morris. "Ruff," barked Candy. She waved her long, bushy tail around.

"Candy, you're a mess. Look at your tail. It's full of stickers," said Morris. He looked down and saw that his socks were full of stickers, too. "Let's go home and I'll comb the stickers out of your fur," he said.

Morris picked the stickers out of his socks. He combed them out of Candy's tail. He took the stickers to his big brother. "Jacob, look what was in Candy's fur!"

"Do you know what those are?" asked Jacob. "Stickers are plant seeds. The hooks stick to animals that pass by. The seeds fall off when the animal rubs against a fence or a tree. They could start to grow in the new place. Let's go outside and plant these stickers. Maybe we can get them to grow."

The boys scattered the stickers in a big pot. Morris covered the stickers with dirt. Jacob sprinkled them with water. "Now we just have to wait," said Jacob.

Name _____

Questions about *Stickers*

1. How did Candy get stickers in her tail?

   _____

2. How did Morris get stickers in his socks?

   _____

3. How did Morris get the stickers out of Candy's tail and his socks?

   _____

4. What did Morris do with the stickers that he took out of Candy's tail?

   _____

5. What part of a plant are stickers?

   _____

6. Why do seeds of some plants have hooks?

   _____

7. What could happen if the stickers landed on the ground?

   _____

8. What do the boys hope will happen to the stickers they planted?

   _____

Name _____

What Happened Next?

Number the sentences in order.

_____ Morris and Jacob planted the stickers.

_____ Morris combed Candy's tail.

_____ Candy ran through the weeds.

_____ Morris showed the stickers to his brother.

_____ Candy got stickers in her tail.

Who Said It?

1. "Do you know what those are?"   _____

2. "Candy, you're a mess."   _____

3. "Ruff."   _____

4. "Look what was in Candy's fur!"   _____

5. "Now we just have to wait."   _____

Name _____

What Does It Mean?

Read the story.
Find the words with these meanings.

1. hair on an animal _____

2. seeds with hooks _____

3. a piece of land with no buildings _____

4. spread something around _____

5. soil _____

6. ran after _____

Circle the correct meaning.

1. In this story, **bark** means
      a. the outside cover of a tree
      b. a kind of candy
      c. the sound a dog makes

2. In this story, **plant** means
      a. a growing thing
      b. to put seeds in the ground
      c. a factory

3. In this story, **stick** means
      a. to hook on to something
      b. a piece of wood from a tree
      c. to paste something to paper

Name _____

Silent Letters

Some words have letters that do not make a sound.

com**b**   tak**e**   **k**now

Read these words.
Circle the letters that do not make a sound.

knock   bomb   write
home   knot   climb

Fill in the missing words.

1. My uncle is going to _____ a mountain.

2. Jai had a _____ in his shoelace.

3. Did you hear a _____ at the door?

4. Kerry is going to _____ a letter to her friend.

Contractions

Write the contractions for these words.

1. cannot _____   4. it is _____   7. there is _____

2. let us _____   5. will not _____   8. is not _____

3. he is _____   6. did not _____   9. could not _____

Word Box		
couldn't	it's	let's
he's	won't	can't
there's	isn't	didn't

       More Read and Understand • Grade 2 • EMC 746

What Will Grow?

Jacob and Morris planted the stickers in a big pot. Imagine you found some strange stickers on your pet. Pretend you have planted the stickers in this pot.

Draw a picture of the stickers.

Draw the plant you think will grow from the strange stickers.

The Country Mouse and the City Mouse

One sunny spring day, City Mouse went to visit his cousin in the country. Country Mouse was happy to see his cousin. He made a bed of straw in the barn. "You can sleep here," he told City Mouse. He gathered seeds. "Here are seeds to eat," said Country Mouse.

"I don't see how you can eat this food," said City Mouse. "And how can you sleep in straw? Come to the city with me and I'll show you how to live."

The two mice set off for town. It was late when they came to the house where City Mouse lived. City Mouse showed his cousin a nest of cotton rags. "This is where we will sleep," he said. "But let's eat before we go to bed."

City Mouse led his cousin to the dining room. Soon the mice were eating bread crusts, peas, and cake. While the mice were eating, danger was coming closer. Suddenly they heard a loud snarl. "It's the cat!" shouted City Mouse.

In the blink of an eye, the cat pounced. The mice scampered off the table and ran into a hole in the wall. Country Mouse could feel his heart pounding. "As soon as the cat is gone, I'm going home."

"Why are you going so soon?" asked City Mouse.

"It's better to eat seeds in a safe place," said Country Mouse, "than to eat cake where there is danger." And off he went.

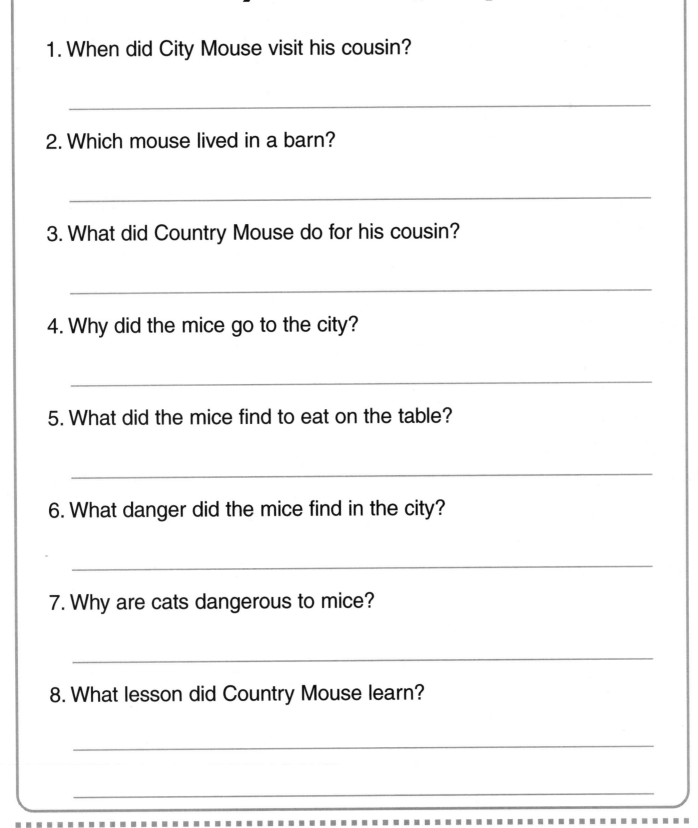

Name _____

Questions about
The Country Mouse and the City Mouse

1. When did City Mouse visit his cousin?

   _____

2. Which mouse lived in a barn?

   _____

3. What did Country Mouse do for his cousin?

   _____

4. Why did the mice go to the city?

   _____

5. What did the mice find to eat on the table?

   _____

6. What danger did the mice find in the city?

   _____

7. Why are cats dangerous to mice?

   _____

8. What lesson did Country Mouse learn?

   _____

Name _____

What Happened Next?

Cut out the sentences below.
Paste them in order.

City Mouse went to visit Country Mouse.

1. [ ]

2. [ ]

3. [ ]

4. [ ]

5. [ ]

6. [ ]

Country Mouse went home.

- ✂ - - - - -

"Come to the city with me," said City Mouse.

Country Mouse made a nest of straw for his cousin.

The cat snarled and pounced on the table.

"How can you eat these seeds?" said City Mouse.

The mice ate bread crusts, peas, and cake in the city.

The mice ran into a hole in the wall.

Name _____

What Does It Mean?

Match:

visit   dried grain stems

straw   your uncle's child

cousin   a place outside of town

scamper   the brown edges of bread

danger   something harmful

crusts   to go to see someone

country   to run

What does **in the blink of an eye** mean?

_____

Draw the picture for each word or words.

City Mouse	Country Mouse
straw	seeds

Name _____

Missing Sounds

Write the missing sounds in these words: **ee**   **ea**

sl_____p   _____t   m_____t

p_____s   s_____ds   thr_____

Write a sentence using each word.

1. _____.

2. _____.

3. _____.

4. _____.

5. _____.

6. _____.

Sounds of C

Read the words.
Write the sound you hear **c** make (**k** or **s**).

1. come _____   4. cereal _____   7. cent _____
2. city _____   5. cat _____   8. country _____
3. cousin _____   6. mice

Who Said It?

Draw lines from each mouse to what he said.

- "Here are seeds to eat."

- "But let's eat before we go to bed."

- "How can you sleep in straw?"

- "I'm going home."

- "Come to the city with me and I'll show you how to live."

- "It's the cat!"

- "It's better to eat seeds in a safe place than to eat cake where there is danger."

- "You can sleep here."

Gilly's Surprise

Gilly loves chickens. She loves the fluffy little chicks and the fat hens. She even loves the noisy rooster with his big tail feathers. Every day Gilly feeds the chickens. She gives them fresh water. She helps her dad clean out the coop and spread new straw. But the job she likes best is gathering the eggs that the hens lay. That is, she liked it best until yesterday.

When Gilly got home from school yesterday, her mother said, "Gilly, will you please gather the hens' eggs for me?" Gilly changed into her play clothes, got her egg basket, and headed for the chicken coop. Each hen had a little wooden box full of straw where she could lay her eggs.

Gilly reached into the first box and pulled out a smooth, warm brown egg. She reached into the second box and pulled out a smooth, warm white egg. She reached into the third box. "Eek!" she yelled, as she dropped a wiggly, furry gray thing. She watched as a wee gray mouse ran through the wire fence and out of the chicken coop.

Gilly ran up to the house. "Mom, Mom, come quick!" shouted Gilly. "It was in the nest. I thought it was an egg, but it was a mouse. Yech! I touched a mouse!"

"Calm down, Gilly. It's all right," said Mom in a quiet voice. "The little mouse was just looking for food. Mice like the chickens' food. Go wash your hands. I'll finish collecting the eggs."

After dinner Gilly's father put a trap in the coop to catch the mouse. "Will the trap hurt the mouse?" asked Gilly.

"No, this trap will catch the mouse alive. We will take it to the cow pasture and let it go," explained her father.

Gilly still gathers the eggs, but she looks into each nest before she picks up anything!

Name _____

Questions about *Gilly's Surprise*

1. Tell four things Gilly did to help take care of the chickens.

   _____

2. What did Mother ask Gilly to do when she got home from school?

   _____

3. What scared Gilly?

   _____

4. What is going to happen to the mouse?

   _____

5. Do you think the mouse will come back? Why?

   _____

   _____

6. How do you think the mouse felt when Gilly picked it up?

   _____

How Did Gilly Feel?

Color the face to show how Gilly felt.

😊 😢 1. when she fed the chickens

😊 😢 2. when she touched the wiggly gray thing

😊 😢 3. when she picked up a smooth warm egg

😊 😢 4. when she saw she was holding a mouse

Name _____

What Happened Next?

Write the sentences in order.

1. _____.

2. _____.

3. _____.

4. _____.

Gilly pulled out a smooth white egg.

Gilly shouted, "Mom, come quick!"

Gilly dropped a wiggly gray mouse.

Gilly pulled out a smooth brown egg.

Counting Syllables

How many syllables do you hear?
Color the pictures.

one syllable—blue   two syllables—green

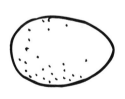

Name _____

What Does It Mean?

Circle the answer.

1. What would you find in a **coop**?
   a. hens
   b. pigs
   c. goats

2. What is a word that means **wee**?
   a. old
   b. wet
   c. tiny

3. How do you feel if you are **calm**?
   a. hungry
   b. quiet
   c. silly

4. What would you do with a **trap**?
   a. cook in it
   b. catch an animal in it
   c. go for a ride in it

5. What grows in a **pasture**?
   a. grass
   b. carrots
   c. roses

Draw the answer.

What was smooth, warm, and brown?

What was wiggly, furry, and gray?

Name _____

What Does the Letter Say?

Write the letter you hear at the end of each word.

by _i_   happy _e_

1. my _____   5. Gilly _____   9. fly _____
2. fluffy _____   6. cry _____   10. wiggly _____
3. shy _____   7. wiggly _____
4. tiny _____   8. why _____

What sound do you hear at the end of the two-syllable words? _____

What sound do you hear at the end of the one-syllable words? _____

What Sound Do You Hear?

These letters make the same sound.

chair   rea**ch**   ma**tch**

Write the missing letters to name these pictures.

_____icken

pea_____

wa_____

wren_____

ma_____

_____ain

Name _____

Chickens

Hen   Chick   Rooster

Write about how to take good care of a flock of chickens.

_____

_____

_____

_____

_____

What Do You Do with an Egg?

Make a list of ways to use an egg.

_____   _____

_____   _____

_____   _____

_____   _____

Circle the way you like eggs best.

Bones

Yolanda loved playing on the monkey bars at recess. One day as she was turning a flip, she fell off. "Ow! My arm hurts," she cried. Yolanda's father came and took her to the hospital.

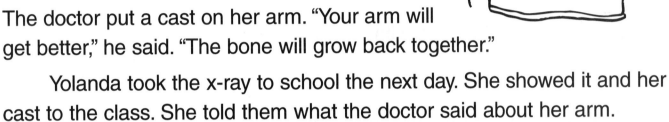

"Yolanda, your arm is broken," the doctor said. He showed her an x-ray of her arm. Yolanda could see the broken bone. The doctor put a cast on her arm. "Your arm will get better," he said. "The bone will grow back together."

Yolanda took the x-ray to school the next day. She showed it and her cast to the class. She told them what the doctor said about her arm.

Her teacher, Mrs. Davis, told the class more about bones. "All of you have many bones. These bones make your skeleton. If you didn't have a skeleton, you would be as saggy as a beanbag. The bones in your skeleton help you move." The recess bell rang. Everyone went out to play.

After recess Mrs. Davis showed the class a picture of a skeleton. "Bones can't bend, so a skeleton has joints. Joints are like the hinges on a door. Joints let your ankles and knees and wrists and elbows bend. You have joints in your jaw, hips, and shoulders, too."

Mrs. Davis told the class many things about their skeletons. She said that good food and exercise help bones grow and stay strong. Then it was time for lunch.

"I'm going to eat my vegetables and drink my milk," said Yolanda. "I want to keep my bones strong."

Name _____

Questions about *Bones*

1. How did Yolanda hurt her arm?

_____

2. How did the doctor know Yolanda's arm was broken?

_____

3. What did the doctor put on Yolanda's arm?

_____

4. What did Yolanda share with the class?

_____

5. How can you keep your skeleton strong?

_____

6. Why do you think Yolanda fell off the monkey bars?

_____

7. How could Yolanda be safer when she plays on the monkey bars?

_____

What About You?

Circle the answers.

Did you ever fall off the monkey bars?   yes   no
Did you ever have an x-ray?   yes   no
Did you ever break a bone?   yes   no

What Happened Next?

Cut out the sentences below.
Paste them in order.

1.

2.

3.

4.

5.

✂ -

The doctor put a cast on Yolanda's arm. "Your arm will get better," he said.

Mrs. Davis told the class about the skeleton.

Yolanda was playing when she fell off the monkey bars.

Yolanda showed the x-ray to her class at school.

The doctor took an x-ray of Yolanda's arm. She had a broken arm.

More Read and Understand • Grade 2 • EMC 746

Bones Crossword Puzzle

Word Box

cast
doctor
hospital
joint
skeleton
skull
x-ray

Across
2. a place to take care of sick and hurt people
4. the bones in your head
6. a person who takes care of sick and hurt people
7. a hard cover to keep a broken bone from moving

Down
1. a picture of your bones
3. all the bones in a body
5. the place where two bones come together and move

Name _____

Long o

Read the words.
Circle the words with the long **o** sound.

broke	bone	throw
doctor	off	move
show	school	some
body	grow	elbow

Fill in the missing words.

1. Yolanda _____ her arm.

2. I bumped my _____ when I fell.

3. How much did you _____ last year?

4. Will you _____ me how to bake a cake?

5. How far can you _____ that ball?

Count Syllables

1. skeleton ___3___   6. together _____

2. places _____   7. every _____

3. bones _____   8. joints _____

4. elbow _____   9. Yolanda _____

5. didn't _____   10. doctor _____

Name _____

Skeleton

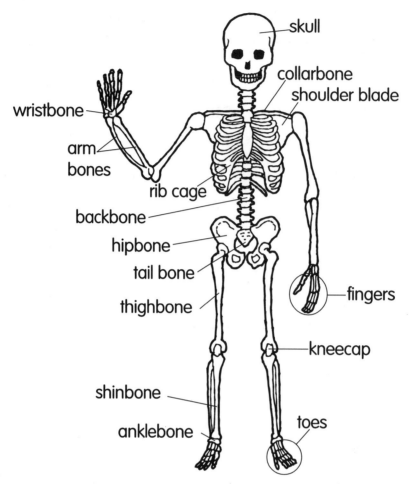

skull

collarbone

shoulder blade

wristbone

arm
bones

rib cage

backbone

hipbone

tail bone

thighbone

fingers

kneecap

shinbone

anklebone

toes

Look at the skeleton.
Name these bones.

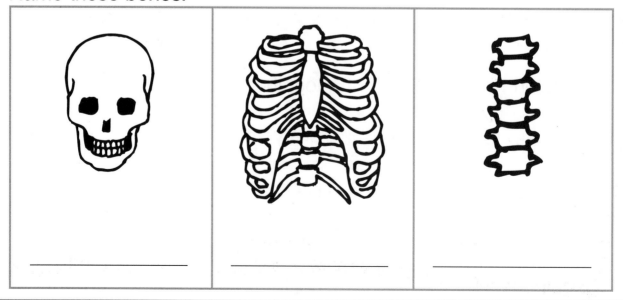

_____   _____   _____

Pen Pals

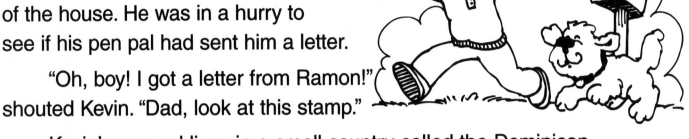

"Kevin," called Father, "Please go pick up the mail." Kevin ran to the mailbox in front of the house. He was in a hurry to see if his pen pal had sent him a letter.

"Oh, boy! I got a letter from Ramon!" shouted Kevin. "Dad, look at this stamp."

Kevin's pen pal lives in a small country called the Dominican Republic. Kevin lives in the state of Maine in the United States. Ramon and Kevin have been writing to each other for a long time.

"I wonder what he's been doing," said Kevin as he opened the envelope. The letter said:

Dear Kevin,

How are you? I am fine. I have been playing baseball with my friends every day after school. I'm the catcher. I wish you could come and play with us.

We are going to a party at my aunt's house on Saturday. She is going to make my favorite chicken stew. It has plantains, chicken, sausage, and vegetables in it. I hope I get a chicken foot in my bowl.

What are you doing?

Your friend,

Ramon

Kevin put the letter back in the envelope and ran upstairs to get a pencil and some paper. He wrote:

Dear Ramon,

Thank you for the letter. I wish I could come and play baseball with you and your friends. I am pitcher on my Little League team this year.

Did you really get a chicken foot in your stew? What does a chicken foot taste like? My grandmother makes chicken stew, too. But her stew has chicken and noodles and gravy. We never eat the feet. I didn't know what a plantain was. My mother told me it is a kind of banana.

Next week is July 4. We are going to have a picnic in the park. When it is dark we will watch the fireworks. Do you ever have picnics and fireworks?

Your friend,
Kevin

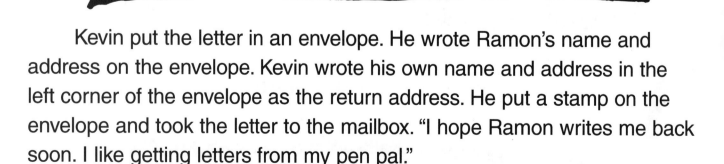

Kevin put the letter in an envelope. He wrote Ramon's name and address on the envelope. Kevin wrote his own name and address in the left corner of the envelope as the return address. He put a stamp on the envelope and took the letter to the mailbox. "I hope Ramon writes me back soon. I like getting letters from my pen pal."

Name _____

Questions about *Pen Pals*

1. Why was Kevin in a hurry to get the mail?

_____

2. Who is Kevin's pen pal and where does he live?

_____

3. What did Kevin want to know about chicken feet?

_____

4. What three things must you put on an envelope before you mail a letter?

_____

5. What does Kevin's family do on the 4th of July?

_____

6. What do pen pals do?

_____

Write the names of the pictures.

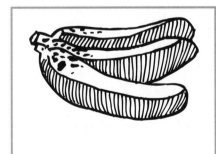

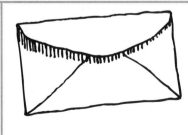

_____   _____   _____

Name _____

What Happened Next?

Cut out the sentences below.
Paste them in order.

1. [ ]

2. [ ]

3. [ ]

4. [ ]

5. [ ]

6. [ ]

✂ -

Put the letter in the mailbox.

Write a letter.

Write the address and the return address on the envelope.

Fold the letter and put it in the envelope.

Put a stamp on the envelope.

Get paper, a pencil, and an envelope.

Name _____

What Does It Mean?

Match to make a sentence.

1. Pen pals	tells where you live.
2. A letter is	a country.
3. Your address	write letters to each other.
4. The United States is	a kind of banana.
5. A plantain is	a message sent by mail.
6. Stew is	meat and vegetables cooked together.

Name the parts of the envelope.

1. _____

2. _____

3. _____

4. _____

Kevin James
112 Elm Street
Brunswick, Maine 04011   **2**   **1**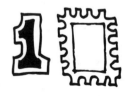

3 Ramon Fernandes
7 Calle del Sol
La Vega
Dominican Republic

Name _____

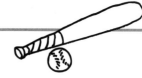

A Word Family—*ew*

Write **ew** on the lines to make a word family.

n_____   d_____   f_____   st_____

gr_____   cr_____   bl_____   fl_____

Read the words you made.
Fill in the missing words.

1. Mother made a pot of _____ for dinner.

2. A flock of birds _____ over the rooftop.

3. Penny is going to buy a _____ dress for the party.

Pen Pals

Pen pals learn a lot about each other from the letters they write. Fill in the chart to show what you learned about Ramon and Kevin from their letters.

	Ramon	Kevin
Where they live		
What they do		
What they eat		

Name _____

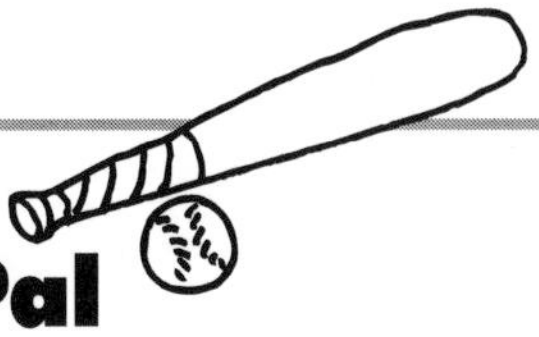

_____'s Pen Pal
(your name)

Pretend you have a pen pal. Write a letter to your pen pal.
Tell about yourself.

Dear _____,

_____

_____

_____

_____

_____

_____

_____

Your friend,

_____

A Peanut Butter Sandwich

"I'm so hungry I could eat an elephant," Billy Joe told his friend Davy. "Let's go see if my grandma will make us a snack." Billy Joe and Davy ran across the school yard and down the street. They knocked on Grandmother's back door.

"Grandma, can we have something to eat?" Billy Joe asked. "I can't make it all the way home without a snack."

Grandmother was putting on her coat and hat. "I don't have time to fix you anything right now. I'm late for my computer class. You boys can fix yourselves a sandwich if you don't make a mess," Grandma said as she headed out the door.

"I like peanut butter," said Davy. "Let's make peanut butter sandwiches."

The boys took out the bread, peanut butter, and a knife. "What do you want with your peanut butter?" asked Billy Joe. "Do you want jam or a banana?"

"A banana! I don't want a banana on my sandwich," said Davy. "I'll take jam. Does your grandma have strawberry jam?"

Billy Joe handed Davy a jar of strawberry jam. "You don't know what you're missing, Davy. Peanut butter, honey, and banana make the best tasting sandwich you ever ate."

Billy Joe spread peanut butter on one slice of bread. He put honey on the other slice. He cut the banana and put it on top of the peanut butter. He put the two slices together and took a big bite. "This is so good. Do you want a bite?" he asked Davy.

Davy made a face and said, "No, thanks. I'll stick to peanut butter and jam. Do you think your grandma would mind if we had some milk? This peanut butter sticks to the roof of my mouth."

The boys drank some milk and ate their sandwiches. Billy Joe put everything away, and Davy washed the dirty dishes.

When Grandmother returned, the boys were playing with her dog. "You boys did a fine job. The kitchen is spotless. Scoot now. It's time you went home." She gave each boy a big hug and sent them on their way.

Name _____

Questions about
A Peanut Butter Sandwich

1. Why did the boys stop at Billy Joe's grandmother's house?

_____

2. Where was his grandmother going?

_____

3. What did Grandmother tell the boys they could do?

_____

4. What kind of sandwich did Billy Joe eat?

_____

5. What kind of sandwich did Davy eat?

_____

6. What did the boys drink with their sandwiches?

_____

7. How did the boys clean up their mess?

_____

8. Why did Grandmother send the boys home?

_____

Name _____

Number the sentences to tell how to make a sandwich.

_____ Open the jar of peanut butter and spread some on one slice of bread.

_____ Put together the slice of bread with honey and the slice of bread with peanut butter and banana. Eat it up!

_____ Take out the bread, peanut butter, honey, banana, and a knife.

_____ Now clean up the mess.

_____ Peel the banana and cut it into slices. Put the banana slices on the peanut butter.

_____ Open the loaf of bread and take out two slices.

_____ Open the jar and put honey on the other slice of bread.

Number the pictures in order.

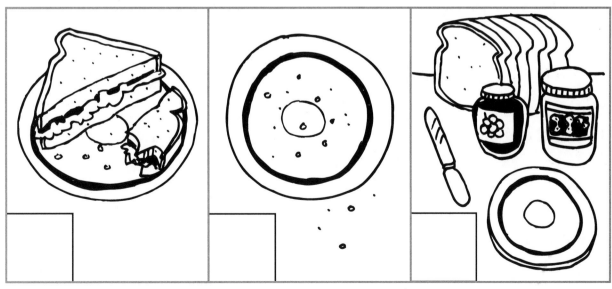

89   More Read and Understand • Grade 2 • EMC 746

Name _____

A Peanut Butter Sandwich Crossword

Word Box

dirty
grandmother
home
hungry
peanut butter
return
slice

Across
4. your parent's mother
5. need to eat
6. a piece of bread
7. to come back

Down
1. a food made of crushed nuts
2. not clean
3. the place you live

What Does It Mean?

Match:
1. could eat an elephant

2. the roof of the mouth

3. scoot now

go away now

top part of the
inside of the mouth

very, very hungry

Name _____

The Sounds of *th*

Circle the words with the sound of **th** in **the**.
Make an **X** on the words with the sound of **th** in **th**ing.

thank	they	them
with	three	think
there	then	teeth

Fill in the missing words.

1. Kim's cat had _____ kittens.

2. _____ are sisters.

3. Put the chair over _____.

4. _____ you for helping me.

5. Pete has lost five _____.

6. I like milk _____ my sandwich.

7. Do you _____ this is a good book?

 More Read and Understand • Grade 2 • EMC 746

Name _____

My Favorite Sandwich

Draw your favorite sandwich on the plate.

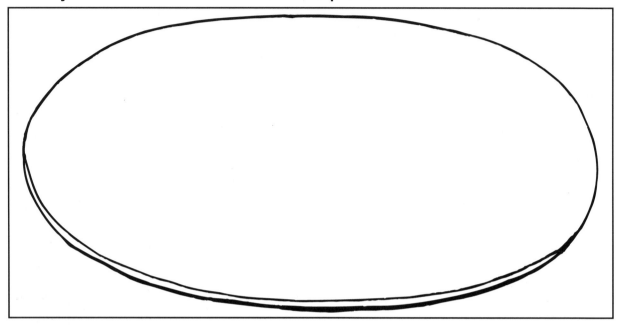

Tell how to make the sandwich.

_____

_____

_____

_____

_____

I like a _____ sandwich because

_____

_____

Down in the Orchard

Down in the orchard
It's harvest time
Up the tall ladders
The fruit pickers climb.

Among green branches
That sway overhead
Apples are hanging
All rosy and red.

Just ripe for picking
All juicy and sweet
Pretty to look at
And tasty to eat.

Anonymous

   Apples and other fruits grow on trees. Farmers grow the fruit your family buys at the supermarket. Many fruit trees grow together in places called orchards.

   If you watched a fruit tree for a while, this is what you would see. Blossoms form on the tree branches. Small, green fruit grows from each blossom. The fruit grows larger until it is ripe. Then the fruit is harvested.

   Sometimes fruit is picked and sent to the supermarket while it is still green. The green fruit ripens during its trip to the supermarket.

Name _____

Questions about *Down in the Orchard*

1. Where is the fruit you buy in a supermarket grown?

   _____

2. What do blossoms change into?

   _____

3. What happens at harvest time?

   _____

4. What happens to fruit that is picked and sent to the supermarket while it is still green?

   _____

5. What are two other fruits that grow on trees?

   _____   _____

Draw these parts of an apple tree.

blossom	fruit

Name _____

What Happens Next?

Draw a picture to show what happens next.

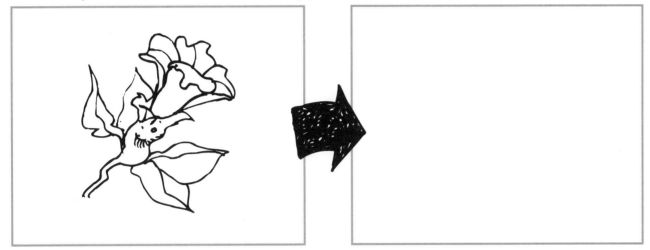

Name _____

What Does It Mean?

Match:

1. orchard   the parts of a tree growing out of the trunk

2. harvest   to swing

3. branches   dirt

4. sway   a flower

5. soil   place where fruit trees are grown

6. blossom   to pick ripe fruit

Use these words in sentences.

         harvest   orchard   blossom

1. _____

_____

2. _____

_____

3. _____

_____

Long-Vowel Words

Read the words.
Write the letter that names the vowel you hear.

1. time _____i_____

2. sweet _____

3. by _____

4. climb _____

5. eat _____

6. goat _____

7. sway _____

8. cube _____

9. green _____

10. ripe _____

11. day _____

12. bone _____

13. rain _____

14. cute _____

What Rhymes?

Read the poem again.
Write the words that rhyme with these words.

1. overhead _____

2. sweet _____

3. time _____

You can change the first letter or letters of a word to make a rhyming word.

bee   **w**ee   **tr**ee

1. took _____ook _____ook

2. tall _____all _____all

3. down _____own _____own

4. sweet _____eet _____eet

An Apple Tree

Name the parts of this tree.

List three ways to use apples.

1. _____

2. _____

3. _____

A Tree House

"Hurray! Hurray! We're going to build a tree house today," shouted Kate and Jake.

An old oak tree grew in the backyard of their new home. There were three low branches that were just right for a tree house.

First came Dad carrying the lumber for the floor, walls, and roof.

Next came Mom carrying a short ladder for climbing up into the tree.

After Mom came Uncle Mike carrying a saw for cutting the lumber.

Then came Kate carrying a can of paint and some brushes to paint the tree house.

Jake came last carrying the toolbox and a bag of nails. They would need these to build the tree house. "We look like a parade!" laughed Jake.

It took all weekend to build the tree house. Everyone helped. They cut the lumber and nailed it in place. They painted it yellow and blue. Mom set the ladder against the tree so that Kate and Jake could climb up into the tree house.

"Wow! We did a great job," said Kate. "Can we sleep in our tree house tonight? We have sleeping bags."

"Not tonight," said Mom. "It's going to rain. You can sleep out when the weather is better." And they did.

Name _____

Questions about *A Tree House*

1. Write was the tree house built?

   _____

2. What did the family use to build the tree house?

   _____   _____   _____

   _____   _____   _____

3. What were these used for?

   lumber   _____

   saw   _____

   nails   _____

   brushes _____

4. How long did it take to build the tree house?

   _____

5. Why didn't Kate and Jake sleep in the tree house as soon as it
   was finished?

   _____

6. Why could they build a tree house at their new home?

   _____

Name _____

What Happened Next?

Write the names in the order they marched to the oak tree.
What did each person carry?

First, _____ carried _____.

Second, _____ carried _____.

Third, _____ carried _____.

Fourth, _____ carried _____.

Last, _____ carried _____.

Who Said It?

1. "We look like a parade!"   _____

2. "We're going to build a tree house."   _____ and

    _____

3. "It's going to rain."   _____

4. "Wow! We did a great job."   _____

Name _____

What Does It Mean?

Write the words under the pictures. You will not use all of the words.

ladder	lumber	sleeping bag
hammer	nails	screwdriver
saw	flashlight	toolbox

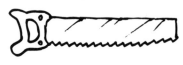

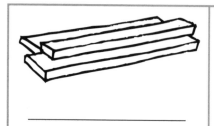

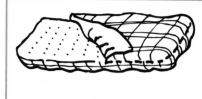

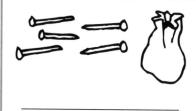

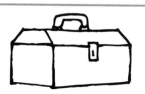

_____   _____   _____

_____   _____   _____

Write sentences using three of the words.

1. _____

2. _____

3. _____

In a Toolbox

Find these tools in the toolbox.

✓ nails   wrench
  hammer   saw
  screwdriver   pliers

```
s c r e w d r i v e r
n a i l s h a m m e r
p l i e r s x s a w z
t u l w r e n c h x y
```

Name _____

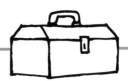

It Says A

Read these long **a** words to a friend.

Jake	say	paint
cake	way	rain
make	stay	train
skate	clay	brain
state	play	wait

Write the missing letters.

ay   **a–e**   **ai**

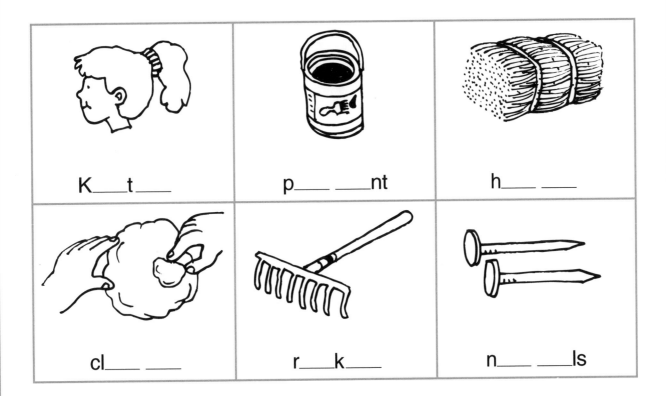

K__t__   p__ __nt   h__ __

cl__ __   r__k__   n__ __ls

Name _____

_____'s Tree House
(your name)

What would you need to build a tree house?

_____   _____

_____   _____

_____   _____

How would you build it?

_____

_____

_____

Draw what it would look like.

Giant Pandas

What is black and white and looks like a big bear? A giant panda! There are very few giant pandas in the world. In the wild, they live in bamboo forests. These forests are found only in parts of China. Some giant pandas are in zoos around the world. These pandas were gifts from China.

Giant pandas can eat bamboo for 12 or more hours a day. That's a lot of bamboo! They have paws with a toe that works like a thumb to grab the bamboo. They have big, strong teeth for chewing bamboo.

Giant pandas are born alive. The babies are very small when they are born. These tiny babies are pink with no hair. Their eyes are closed. As they grow, the young pandas get black spots on their skin. Panda mothers feed and protect their babies for many months.

China wants to protect the giant pandas living in the bamboo forests. Land has been set aside where giant pandas can live safe from harm. Someday there may be many more pandas in the world.

Name _____

Questions about *Giant Pandas*

1. What do giant pandas look like?

_____

2. Where do wild giant pandas live?

_____

3. How do these help a giant panda eat bamboo?

_____   _____

_____   _____

4. What are newborn pandas like?

_____

5. How do you know giant pandas are good mothers?

_____

6. Why are pandas safer in China now?

_____

Name _____

A Giant Panda Is Born

Cut out the sentences below and paste them in order.

Start here

At one month, the baby gets black spots on its skin.	When it is grown, a giant panda is big. It has black-and-white fur.
At four months, the baby has hair. Its eyes are open. It can crawl.	When it is born, a panda has no hair. Its eyes are not open.

Name _____

Giant Pandas Crossword Puzzle

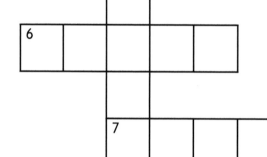

Word Box

bamboo
chew
China
giant panda
hair
harm
protect
teeth
tiny

Across
1. to break up food with your teeth
2. the coat of an animal
3. a large black-and-white animal
5. a kind of plant
6. more than one tooth
7. very small

Down
1. the name of a country
2. to hurt something
4. to keep safe

More Read and Understand • Grade 2 • EMC 746

Name _____

The Sounds of G

Read the words.
Write the sound the letter **g** makes (**g** or **j**).

1. get   _____   5. gum   _____

2. giant   _____   6. giraffe   _____

3. gem   _____   7. game   _____

4. gift   _____   8. gingerbread _____

It Starts with *gr*

Write **gr** on each line to make a word.
Read the words you make.

_____ow   _____ape   _____een

_____ab   _____ass   _____andmother

Fill in the missing words.

1. Baby pandas _____ very fast.

2. Dad cut the _____ _____ in the
   front yard.

3. _____ made jars of _____ jam.

Name _____

Is It a Giant Panda?

Circle the answer.

1. black-and-white fur	yes	no
2. feathers	yes	no
3. strong teeth	yes	no
4. strong beak	yes	no
5. eats bamboo	yes	no
6. four legs	yes	no
7. two legs	yes	no
8. lays eggs	yes	no
9. has a tiny, hairless baby	yes	no
10. found wild in China	yes	no

What Am I?
Look at your "no" answers. Draw that kind of animal.

Stone Soup

One cool autumn day, a hiker knocked on a farmer's door. When the farmer opened the door, the hiker said, "I am lost and I ran out of food yesterday."

"I don't give food to strangers," said the stingy farmer with a scowl.

"You don't understand," said the hiker. "I don't need your food. I just want to borrow that large stone in your garden. I need to fill my pot with water, too."

The farmer said, "I don't see anything wrong with that. I guess you can have the stone and some water."

The hiker washed the dirt off the stone. He put the stone into his pot. He filled the pot with water and set it on a small campfire. Soon the water was boiling. The farmer's wife came to see what was going on. She peeked in the pot. "I've never seen anyone make soup out of a stone and water," she said.

"You should try it. It makes wonderful soup," said the hiker. "It's even better with onions."

"Well, I guess I could give you an onion," said the farmer's wife. She went to the farmhouse and got an onion. The hiker put the onion into the pot. He waited for the stone soup to cook.

The farmer's oldest daughter came out to see what was going on. "I've never seen anyone make soup out of a stone and water," she said.

The hiker told her how good the soup was going to be. "It's even better with carrots," he said.

"Well, I guess I can give you some carrots," said the farmer's daughter. She went to the garden and pulled up some carrots. While she was there she got some celery, too.

The hiker put the carrots and celery into the pot. He waited for the soup to cook. The farmer's youngest son came to see what was going on. "I've never seen my mother make soup with a stone and water," he said.

The hiker said, "Can't you smell how good it is? It's even better with potatoes."

"I know where there are some potatoes," said the farmer's son. "I'll get you some." He ran to the potato patch and dug up three potatoes for the soup.

The hiker put the potatoes into the pot. The good smell of the soup filled the air. "This soup is almost done," he said. "Go ask your folks if they would like to have a bowl of soup with me."

The farmer's son ran to the farmhouse to give his parents the message. Soon the whole family came running out with bowls and spoons. The farmer even brought out a loaf of bread.

The hiker thanked them for their help and asked how to get to the next town. Whistling merrily, he walked down the road.

After the hiker left, the farmer picked up the stone and gave it to his wife. "Here, wife, use this stone the next time you make soup."

Name _____

Questions about *Stone Soup*

1. Where did the hiker get the stone and the water to put into the soup pot?

   _____

2. Where did the farmer's wife get the onion?

   _____

3. Where did the daughter get the carrots?

   _____

4. Where did the son get the potatoes?

   _____

5. What message did the hiker send to the farmer and his family?

   _____

6. Why did the farmer give the stone to his wife when the hiker left?

   _____

   _____

7. How did the hiker trick the farmer and his family?

   _____

   _____

Name _____

What Happened Next?

Number the sentences in order.

The hiker made soup.

_____ He put carrots and celery into the pot.

_____ He put potatoes into the pot.

_____ He put an onion into the pot.

_____ He put a stone into the pot.

_____ He filled the pot with water.

The hiker and the farmer's family ate the soup.

In a Soup Pot

Find these things that could be put into a pot of vegetable soup.

Word Box	
beans	peas
✓broth	pepper
carrot	potato
celery	salt
corn	tomato
onion	

```
p  o  t  a  t  o  c  s  p
c  b  e  a  n  s  a  a  e
o  b  r  o  t  h  r  l  p
r  x  p  e  a  s  r  t  p
n  o  n  i  o  n  o  r  e
c  e  l  e  r  y  t  m  r
z  t  o  m  a  t  o  l  x
```

Name _____

What Does It Mean?

Write the word by its meaning.

1. words sent from one person to another _____

2. parents _____

3. a person walking from place to place _____

4. not right _____

5. an angry look _____

6. a married woman _____

7. bread baked in one large piece _____

8. the season after summer _____

<table>
<tr><td>hiker</td><td>wrong</td><td>autumn</td><td>scowl</td></tr>
<tr><td>message</td><td>loaf</td><td>folks</td><td>wife</td></tr>
</table>

Same Meaning

Match the words that mean the same.

1. stone	little
2. merrily	selfish
3. peeked	soil
4. stingy	looked
5. small	rock
6. dirt	happily

Name _____

Add an Ending

	er	est
1. old	_____	_____
2. young	_____	_____
3. tall	_____	_____
4. fast	_____	_____
5. cold	_____	_____
6. soft	_____	_____

Fill in the missing words.

1. My brother is two years _____ than me.

2. Who was the _____ runner at the track meet?

3. My sweater is _____ than my jacket.

4. Jeff is the _____ boy in my class.

Count the Syllables

How many syllables do you hear?

1. stone	__1__	5. anything	_____	9. bowls	_____
2. yesterday	_____	6. guess	_____	10. celery	_____
3. better	_____	7. youngest	_____	11. wonderful	_____
4. onions	_____	8. done	_____	12. whistle	_____

 More Read and Understand • Grade 2 • EMC 746

A Recipe for _____ Soup
(kind of soup)

This is what I would put in my soup.

_____

_____

_____

_____

This is how I would make it.

_____

_____

_____

_____

This is what a bowl of
my soup would look like.

Beavers at Work

Beavers are interesting animals. They change the habitat in which they live. Beavers do this by blocking up streams to make ponds. Then they build their homes, called lodges, in these ponds.

A beaver's body helps it work underwater. It can close off its nose, ears, and throat to keep water out. A beaver can stay underwater for 15 minutes while it is working. A beaver has see-through eyelids so it can see underwater.

A beaver uses its broad, flat tail for steering in the water. Its webbed back feet help the beaver swim. Strong front paws with sharp claws help the beaver dig and carry. It uses its two large orange teeth to gnaw down trees.

Beavers work together to build a dam. First they cut down trees with their big, strong teeth. Next they gnaw the trees into smaller pieces and drag them into the water. The beavers then push stones on top of the logs to keep them from floating away. They use their front paws to scoop up mud to fill in the spaces between the logs.

Water collects behind the dam and makes a pond. The beavers check for leaks and make repairs to the dam when they are needed.

Then the beavers build their home in the pond. The lodge looks like a giant pile of sticks from the outside. It is hollow inside. There is a ledge above the water level where the beavers can sleep. The door to the lodge is underwater.

Name _____

Questions about *Beavers at Work*

1. How do beavers change their habitat?

   _____

2. Tell how each of these things help a beaver build a dam:

   a. see-through eyelids   _____

   b. broad tails   _____

   c. strong paws with claws   _____

   d. large orange teeth   _____

3. How long can a beaver stay underwater?

   _____

4. What do beavers use to keep the logs from floating away?

   _____

5. What does a beaver's lodge look like?

   _____

6. How is a beaver like a human builder?

   _____

Name _____

What Happened Next?

Number the sentences in order.

_____ The beavers push stones on top of the logs so they won't float away.

_____ Water collects behind the dam and makes a pond.

_____ The beavers cut down trees with their big, strong teeth.

_____ They scoop mud to fill in the spaces between the logs.

_____ They gnaw the trees into smaller pieces and drag them into the water.

_____ The beavers build a lodge in the pond.

A Beaver

Follow these directions.
1. Color the beaver's fur brown and its teeth orange.
2. Draw a flat tail on the beaver.
3. Draw a branch in the beaver's paw.
4. Draw a pile of sticks next to the beaver.

What Does It Mean?

Match:

1. habitat   a pool of water

2. lodge   to chew on something

3. pond   the natural place an animal lives

4. gnaw   to fix something that is broken

5. repair   empty in the center

6. hollow   a beaver's home

- -

Fill in the missing words.

1. A beaver's _____ must have trees and a stream.

2. Beavers can _____ tree branches into smaller pieces of wood.

3. Beavers live in a _____ built in a pond.

4. A beaver lodge is _____ in the middle.

Name _____

It Says *E*

Read these long **e** words to a friend.

he	beaver	see
leak	teeth	mean
fifteen	be	stream
we	three	leak

Write the missing letters: **e**   **ea**   **ee**

b____ver	t____th	w____
fift____n	h____	str____m

What Does a Beaver Look Like?

Write a word on each line to describe a beaver.

1. A beaver has a _____, _____ tail.

2. A beaver has two _____ _____ teeth.

3. A beaver's paws have _____ claws.

Name _____

Animal Builders

Read, cut, and paste to answer the riddles.

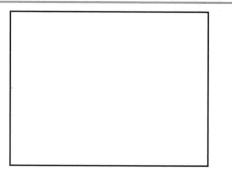

I make a **nest** of twigs and grass.
I lay eggs in the nest.
What am I?

I build a **burrow** underground. I
make tunnels for moving around. I
make rooms to live in. What am I?

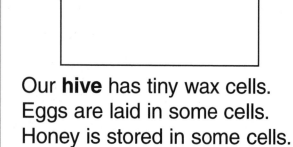

Our **hive** has tiny wax cells.
Eggs are laid in some cells.
Honey is stored in some cells.
What are we?

I make a **web** of silk. When an
insect lands on the web it gets
stuck. This is how I catch my
food. What am I?

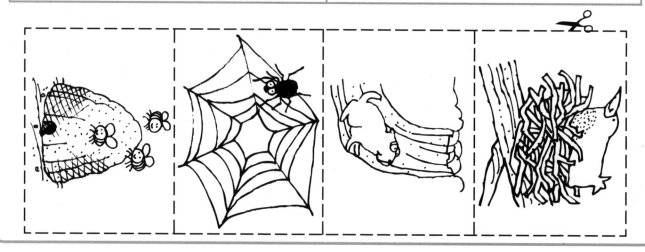

124

Noises in the Night

Jamal sat up in bed. What was that noise on the roof? It sounded like footsteps. Was someone trying to break into the house? "Mom! Dad!" shouted Jamal as he ran into his parents' bedroom. "Did you hear that noise? What is it?"

His dad listened. "I think I know what it is," he said as he grabbed a flashlight and started for the door.

Just then there was a terrible noise in the backyard. "Crash! Bang!" Something had been knocked over. Dad hurried into the backyard. "I was right," said Dad. A large, furry animal was sitting next to the overturned garbage can. Dad turned the flashlight up to the rooftop. There was another large, furry animal. "Scat, you pesky raccoons!" shouted Dad as he flashed the light at them. In the wink of an eye, the raccoon was down off the roof. The raccoons raced out of the yard.

As Jamal helped clean up the mess, his dad told him about their pesky visitors. "Raccoons are wild animals. They come into town trying to find food. Raccoons use their paws like hands. They can take the lid off the garbage can to look for food. Tomorrow we will put hooks on the lid. That should keep it in place if the raccoons come back," said Dad.

"Raccoons look cute, but they can be dangerous," warned Dad. "Never feed one or try to pet it. If you see one in the yard, get Mom or me to take care of it. Now let's go back to bed and get some sleep."

Name _____

Questions about *Noises in the Night*

1. What made Jamal wake up?

_____

2. What did Jamal think was on the roof?

_____

3. What was the noise in the backyard?

_____

4. How did Dad get rid of the animals?

_____

5. How can a raccoon take the lid off a garbage can?

_____

6. What did Dad plan to do to keep raccoons out of the garbage?

_____

7. Why should you never touch a wild animal?

_____

Night Noises

Write about a time noises woke you up in the night.

_____

_____

Name _____

What Happened Next?

Cut out the sentences below.
Paste them in order.

Jamal sat up in bed.

1.

2.

3.

4.

5.

6.

"Now let's go back to bed and get some sleep."

- ✂

He heard a noise on the roof.

There was a terrible noise in the backyard.

"Tomorrow we will get hooks to keep the garbage can shut."

Jamal helped clean up the mess.

He ran to his parents' room.

Dad took a flashlight to the backyard. He scared off
the raccoons.

Name _____

What Does It Mean?

Circle the answer.

1. Where would you find a **roof**?
    a. in a garden
    b. under a car
    c. on top of a house

2. Where do **wild** animals live?
    a. in the library
    b. in a forest
    c. in your bedroom

3. How fast would **in the wink of an eye** be?
    a. in about an hour
    b. slowly
    c. very fast

4. Who are your **parents**?
    a. aunt and uncle
    b. brother and sister
    c. mother and father

5. What could you find in **garbage**?
    a. scraps of food and trash
    b. nickels and dimes
    c. milk and cookies

6. Which one of these would be **terrible**?
    a. a surprise party
    b. a broken arm
    c. a new tooth

Name _____

Sounds of *oo*

Read these words.
Write them under the words with the same **oo** sound.

shook	boot	moon	stood
soon	school	took	room
cook	wood	noon	book

food	look
_____ _____	_____ _____
_____ _____	_____ _____
_____ _____	_____ _____

A Word Family—*ight*

Write one of these letters in front of **ight** to make a word family.

f   l   n   r   s   t

_____ight   _____ight   _____ight

_____ight   _____ight   _____ight

Write sentences using three of your words.

1. _____

2. _____

3. _____

Name _____

Word Endings

Add endings to these words.

help   help<u>ed</u>   help<u>ing</u>

ed   **ing**

1. shout _____   _____

2. start _____   _____

3. knock _____   _____

Double the final consonant and add an ending.

plan   plan**n**<u>ed</u>   plan**n**<u>ing</u>

1. pin _____   _____

2. trap _____   _____

3. beg _____   _____

Fill in the missing words.

1. Jamal was _____, "Did you hear that noise?"

2. The raccoon _____ over the garbage can.

3. The wild animal was _____ in a cage.

Name _____

Noises in the Night

1. Make a circle around the raccoon on the roof.
2. Make an **X** on the raccoon knocking over the garbage can.
3. Draw garbage coming out of the can.
4. Color the light from the flashlight yellow.
5. Write what Dad is saying in the speech bubble.
6. Draw one more raccoon hiding somewhere in the picture.

City Sounds

One sunny afternoon, Carlos sat on the front step of his apartment house. This is what he heard.

Girls laughed and sang as they played jump rope on the sidewalk.

Boys shouted and joked as they played ball in the vacant lot on the corner.

Babies cried and cooed as mothers pushed strollers down the street.

Families walked and talked to friends. They stopped to buy ice cream from the cart on the corner.

Buses, taxis, and cars honked as they drove up and down the street.

Suddenly everyone stopped!

What was that? A siren sounded in the distance. Soon a fire truck raced by.

The street was quiet for a minute. Then the city sounds began again.

Questions about *City Sounds*

1. When did Carlos sit on the front step?

   _____

2. What were they doing?

   a. babies   _____

   b. girls   _____

   c. families   _____

   d. boys   _____

   e. mothers   _____

   f. buses, taxis, and cars _____

3. Why did everyone suddenly stop?

   _____

4. Why did the fire truck race down the street?

   _____

Pronouns

Write a pronoun for each noun.

1. girls _____   4. Carlos _____   7. apartment _____

2. bus   _____   5. boy   _____   8. babies   _____

3. mother _____   6. Sue and I _____

133   More Read and Understand • Grade 2 • EMC 746

Name _____

What Happened Next?

Write the sentences in order.

1. _____

2. _____

3. _____

4. _____

Suddenly everyone stopped.
A fire truck raced by.
The city sounds began again.
Carlos sat on the front step and watched people going by.

Draw what happened next.

Name _____

What Does It Mean?

Match:

1. apartment   a loud sound used as a warning

2. vacant lot   something special

3. stroller   a place to live

4. siren   a vehicle for moving a baby around

5. cooing   an empty area of land

6. treat   a happy sound made by a baby

What Happened?

Circle the words that tell what happened.

buy	race	trucks	what
sat	ice cream	talk	joke
watch	✓ laugh	shout	push
car	walk	stop	play
listen	sing	drove	family

Find the words you circled.

```
w  a  t  c  h  l  i  s  t  e  n
b  d  r  o  v  e  s  t  a  l  k
u  l  a  u  g  h  a  o  w  j  s
y  r  a  c  e  x  t  p  e  o  i
s  h  o  u  t  p  u  s  h  k  n
p  l  a  y  q  w  a  l  k  e  g
```

Name _____

Add an Ending

Add the endings to these words.

	ly	er
slow	_____	_____
quiet	_____	_____
soft	_____	_____
quick	_____	_____

Fill in the missing endings.

1. Sudden_____ it started to rain.

2. A turtle is slow_____ than a rabbit.

3. My sister is old_____ than I am.

4. Speak quiet_____ in the library.

5. Ernest can run fast_____ than Jim.

Do—Did

Match:

eat	drove
go	sat
sit	rode
laugh	went
drive	laughed
ride	ate

Name _____

From My Front Step

Draw and write about what you would see and hear if you sat on your front step.

More Read and Understand • Grade 2 • EMC 746

Answer Key

Note: The level of your students will determine whether or not you require that answers be in the form of complete sentences.

Page 5
1. Alex has a cat and a goldfish.
2. He called Stan's name. He shook the food box.
3. Stan was watching Goldie swim around in her bowl of water.
4. He put Goldie in a new bowl with a wire lid.
5. Stan would have pulled Goldie out of the bowl. Stan would have eaten Goldie.
6. Answers will vary.

Page 6
Stan didn't come when Alex shook his food box.
Stan was sitting on the table watching Goldie.
Stan put a paw into the bowl of water.
"Scat, cat!" yelled Alex.
Stan took off like a flash and hid under the sofa.
Goldie lives in a home with a wire lid across the top.

Page 7
1. naughty — a cover for a box or a dish
2. bowl — an animal's foot
3. wire — to take hold of suddenly
4. paw — a thin piece of metal
5. grab — not behaving well
6. lid — a kind of deep dish

1. b
2. a
3. c

Page 8
1. Alex, Max   5. next
2. mixer   6. box
3. fox   7. fix
4. exit

1. hat, cat, that   (Words will vary.)
2. you, new, blue
3. raw, draw, claw
4. dad, had, glad

Page 11
1. He saw that something was eating his lettuce.
2. He used a box, a stick, and some string.
3. He saw the lettuce leaves wiggle. He saw a pink nose and two eyes.
4. Tony built a pen for Boots in the backyard.
5. come when her name was called,

use the cat's litter box, take treats from someone's hand, stand on her back legs
6. Emma named the rabbit Boots because her white feet looked like she was wearing boots.

Page 12
"Something is eating up my garden," said Tony.
Tony set his trap over a big, green lettuce plant.
Tony reached under the box and lifted out the little pest.
When Emma got to the garden, she saw a furry rabbit.
Boots was a good pet. She came when Tony called her name.
Boots never went into the garden to eat Tony's lettuce again.

Page 13
1. a
2. b
3. b
4. a

1. he   6. well
2. out   7. front
3. went   8. go
4. bad   9. big
5. full   10. untie

Page 14
1. ck   6. k
2. k   7. c
3. c   8. ck
4. c   9. k
5. ck   10. K and ck

Tony's (lettuce)
Emma's (apron)
Ruff's (bone)
rabbit's (carrot)
Ramon's (mitt)
Lee's (wagon)

Page 15
1. he saw something was eating his lettuce.
2. he set a trap to catch the pest.
3. he caught a rabbit.
4. he gently took the rabbit out of the trap OR when he took care of the rabbit.
5. the rabbit didn't eat his plants anymore OR he had a new pet.

Page 18
1. A hen, duck, cat, dog, and some chicks lived on the farm.
2. She planted the seeds. She harvested the seeds. She took the seeds to the mill. She baked bread.
3. They all said "I won't."
4. She wouldn't let them eat the bread because they did not help do the work.
5. Wee, small, and little all mean not big.
6 & 7. Answers will vary.

Page 19
2 4
5 1
3 6

Page 20
1. oven
2. fetch
3. nap
4. flea
5. mill
6. harvest

_✓_ A hen can talk.
_✗_ A hen can eat seeds and bugs.
_✓_ A hen can bake bread.
_✓_ A hen can plant seeds.
_✗_ A hen can live on a farm.
_✗_ A hen can run.

Page 21
grasshopper   bread   tree
broom   train   grapes

1. didn't   4. won't
2. I'll   5. can't
3. it's   6. I'm

Page 22
All but the following words should be circled:
chick, seed, farm, run, pond

big black dog
little red hen
small yellow cat
wee brown duck
hot brown bread

1. wee brown duck
2. big black dog
3. small yellow cat
4. Little Red Hen

Page 25
1. The triplets went into the backyard.
2. Pat–grasshopper, Pete–butterfly, Pam–ant
3. They found the spider in the corner of the porch roof.
4. It had eight legs and two body parts, and it didn't have wings.
5. They are all insects.
6. Animals that talk are make-believe.

fly

Page 26
The triplets went into the backyard.
Pat saw a big brown grasshopper.
Pam saw a tiny red ant.
Pete saw a pretty orange butterfly.
Pete said, "Look up there."
A spider was hanging from a big web.

Page 27
1. grin
2. triplets
3. web
4. porch
5. creepy
6. spider

1. big brown grasshopper
2. pretty orange butterfly
3. tiny red ant
4. shiny black spider

Page 28
door<u>kn</u>ob   <u>kn</u>ee   <u>kn</u>ife
1. aunt
2. ate
3. heard
4. new
5. knew
6. eight

Page 29

	spider	insect
8 legs	X	
6 legs		X
3 body parts		X
2 body parts	X	
no wings	X	
wings		X

Page 31
1. Will ran home.
2. Will wanted to see if his grandfather was there.
3. Will and his grandfather were going ice fishing.
4. Mother was cooking when Will got home.
5. They went by snowmobile because there was ice and snow everywhere.
6. Will was thinking about going fishing.

snowmobile   parka

Page 32
2
6
3
5
1
4

Pictures will vary, but could show Will catching a fish or Grandfather cooking fish.

Page 33
1. teacher — a person who helps you learn
2. soon — in a short time from now
3. kitchen — a room where food is cooked
4. laugh — to make happy sounds
5. frozen — to become hard or solid because of cold

1. He was thinking of something else.
2. Don't be in such a hurry.

These compound words can be in any order on the lines:
grandfather   cowboy
butterfly   baseball
snowmobile   popcorn

Page 34
These words should be circled:
Will   sat   desk   his   fun
must   yet   stop   ran
on

<u>ed</u>	<u>d</u>	<u>t</u>
wanted	filled	looked
shouted	played	walked
painted	jiggled	raced
lifted	pulled	wished
planted	named	laughed

Page 35
1. hear
2. son
3. read
4. buy
5. beat
6. blew

1. it   5. we
2. she   6. it
3. he   7. he
4. they   8. it

Page 37
1. Eric likes the bathtub best.
2. He screams when Mother pulls him out of the tub.
3. They keep the door shut so Eric can't get into the bathtub.
4. Eric reached up and turned the doorknob.
5. Father put a lock on the door and put the key where Eric can't reach it.
6. Eric could get hurt. OR Eric could drown in the water.

Page 38
5 4
2 6
1 3

Page 39
1. pajamas   5. scream
2. brother   6. key
3. empty   7. yanked
4. lock   8. alone

1. pajamas   2. bath

Page 40
1. tub
2. bit
3. cane
4. tube
5. bite
6. can

1. empty   5. little
2. shut   6. ask
3. boy   7. in
4. there   8. over

Page 41
Answers will vary, but could include:
alike–both have water; both are places to wash up; both are places to get clean
different—stand up in a shower; sit in a tub; fill a tub with water; water runs out of a shower

Page 43
1. Masumi had a picnic.
2. Five friends came to the party.
3. The table was set with balloons, funny hats, and sacks.

4. They had sushi, hot dogs, potato chips, and pink lemonade.
5. They played on the swings, slide, and teeter-totter.
6. They looked in the sacks after they ate birthday cake. OR They opened the sacks after Masumi opened her presents.
7. She said it was the best party she ever had.

Page 44
Masumi invited five friends to a picnic.
Masumi's friends came to Green Park.
They ate sushi and drank pink lemonade. There were hot dogs and potato chips, too.
They played on the swings, slide, and teeter-totter.
They had birthday cake and Masumi opened her presents.
Masumi's friends opened the sacks.
"Thank you, Masumi," they said.
Everyone went home with a balloon, a funny hat, and a surprise in a sack.
"This was the best party I ever had," Masumi told her mother.

Page 45
teeter-totter	sack	friend
picnic	balloon	hat
lunch	sushi	lemonade

Page 46
These words should be circled:
place	name	plate	table
came	stay	Saturday	played

Do	Did
drink	drank
see	saw
sit	sat
swing	swung
slide	slid
eat	ate

Page 47
surprises for her friends
a brush and paints
jacks and a ball
a red ribbon
a book

Page 49
1. A cloud is made of tiny drops of water.
2. Snow is made when water drops freeze.
3. Snowflakes fall when they get big and heavy.
4. six sides
   flat
   cold
5. Snow melts on warm ground.
6. Snow covers cold ground.

Page 50
The clouds are full of water drops. The water freezes. Now snowflakes fall. Snow is on the ground and trees. The snow is melting in the hot sun.

Page 51
1. snow
2. freeze
3. cloud
4. lacy
5. melt
6. race
7. sled
8. alike

1. $\bar{o}$	6. ow
2. ow	7. $\bar{o}$
3. ow	8. ow
4. $\bar{o}$	9. $\bar{o}$
5. $\bar{o}$	10. ow

Page 52
cl<u>ou</u>d	cl<u>ow</u>n	m<u>ou</u>se
c<u>ow</u>	fl<u>ow</u>er	h<u>ou</u>se

water	w<u>or</u>m	f<u>er</u>n
butt<u>er</u>	danc<u>er</u>	col<u>or</u>
flav<u>or</u>	flow<u>er</u>	doct<u>or</u>

Sentences will vary.

Page 55
1. Candy ran through the weeds.
2. Morris chased Candy through the weeds.
3. Morris combed Candy's tail. He picked the stickers out of his socks.
4. Morris showed the stickers to his brother.
5. Stickers are seeds.
6. The hooks stick to things. OR The hooks help seeds move to a new place.
7. The stickers could grow into a plant.
8. They hope the stickers will grow.

Page 56
5		1. Jacob
3		2. Morris
1		3. Candy
4		4. Morris
2		5. Jacob

Page 57
1. fur	1. bark–c
2. stickers	2. plant–b
3. vacant lot	3. stick—a
4. scattered	
5. dirt	
6. chased	

Page 58
These letters should be circled:
k b w
e k b

1. climb
2. knot
3. knock
4. write

1. can't	4. it's	7. there's
2. let's	5. won't	8. isn't
3. he's	6. didn't	9. couldn't

Page 61
1. City Mouse visited his cousin one sunny spring day.
2. Country Mouse lived in a barn.
3. Country Mouse made a straw bed and gathered seeds for his cousin.
4. City Mouse wanted to show Country Mouse the good things he had in the city.
5. The mice ate bread crusts, peas, and cake.
6. A cat was the danger in the city.
7. Cats can kill and eat mice.
8. Country Mouse learned that it is better to eat seeds where it is safe than to have fancy food where it is dangerous.

Page 62
Country Mouse made a nest of straw for his cousin.
"How can you eat these seeds?" said City Mouse.
"Come to the city with me," said City Mouse.
The mice ate bread crusts, peas, and cake in the city.
The cat snarled and pounced on the table.
The mice ran into a hole in the wall.

Page 63

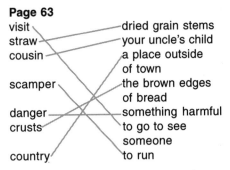

visit — to go to see someone
straw — dried grain stems
cousin — your uncle's child
scamper — to run
danger — something harmful
crusts — the brown edges of bread
country — a place outside of town

In the blink of an eye means very fast.

Page 64

sleep	eat	meat
peas	seeds	three

1. k   5. k
2. s   6. s
3. k   7. s
4. s   8. k

Page 65

City Mouse said:
"But let's eat before we go to bed."
"How can you sleep in straw?"
"Come to the city with me and I'll show you how to live."
"It's the cat!"

Country Mouse said:
"Here are seeds to eat."
"I'm going home."
"It's better to eat seeds in a safe place than to eat cake where there is danger."
"You can sleep here."

Page 68

1. Answers will vary, but should include these:
   She fed the chickens.
   She gave the chickens water.
   She cleaned out the coop.
   She spread straw.
2. Mother asked Gilly to gather the eggs.
3. Gilly was scared when she picked up a mouse.
4. If the mouse comes back it will get caught in the trap.
5. Answers could be "yes" or "no," but must give a reason that makes sense.
6. Answers will vary, but should give the feeling that the mouse was afraid.

1. (happy face)
2. (unhappy face)
3. (happy face)
4. (unhappy face)

Page 69

Gilly pulled out a smooth brown egg.
Gilly pulled out a smooth white egg.
She dropped a wiggly gray mouse.
Gilly shouted, "Mom, come quick!"

egg-blue
rooster-green
feather-green
straw-blue
basket-green
mouse-blue

Page 70

1. a   5. a
2. c
3. b   egg
4. b   mouse

Page 71

1. i   6. i
2. e   7. e
3. i   8. i
4. e   9. i
5. e   10. e

e
i

chicken	peach	watch
wrench	match	chain

Page 74

1. Yolanda fell off the monkey bars.
2. The doctor took an x-ray of her arm.
3. The doctor put a cast on Yolanda's arm.
4. She shared the x-ray and her cast.
5. Good food and exercise keep your skeleton strong.
6. Answers will vary, but could include:
   She was being silly.
   Someone pushed her.
   She slipped.
7. Answers will vary, but could include:
   She will hold on tighter.
   She will watch where she puts her feet.
   She won't do tricks.

Page 75

Yolanda was playing when she fell off the monkey bars.
The doctor took an x-ray of Yolanda's arm. She had a broken arm.
The doctor put a cast on Yolanda's arm. "Your arm will get better," he said.
Yolanda showed the x-ray to her class at school.

Mrs. Davis told the class about the skeleton.

Page 76

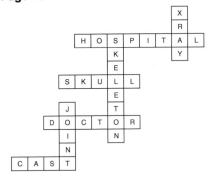

Page 77

These words should be circled:
broke   bone   throw
show   grow   elbow

1. broke   4. show
2. elbow   5. throw
3. grow

1. 3   6. 3
2. 2   7. 2
3. 1   8. 1
4. 2   9. 3
5. 2   10. 2

Page 78

skull   rib cage   backbone

Page 81

1. Kevin was looking for a letter from his pen pal.
2. Ramon is Kevin's pen pal and he lives in the Dominican Republic.
3. He wanted to know if chicken feet taste good.
4. You must put an address, a return address, and a stamp on the envelope.
5. Kevin's family has a picnic and fireworks on the 4th of July.
6. Pen pals write letters to each other.

plantains, chicken foot, envelope

Page 82

Get paper, a pencil, and an envelope.
Write a letter.
Fold the letter and put it in the envelope.
Write the address and the return address on the envelope.
Put a stamp on the envelope.
Put the letter in the mailbox.

Page 83
1. Pen pals write letters to each other.
2. A letter is a message sent by mail.
3. Your address tells where you live.
4. The United States is a country.
5. A plantain is a kind of banana.
6. Stew is meat and vegetables cooked together.

1. stamp
2. return address
3. address
4. envelope

Page 84
n<u>ew</u>   d<u>ew</u>   f<u>ew</u>   st<u>ew</u>
gr<u>ew</u>   cr<u>ew</u>   bl<u>ew</u>   fl<u>ew</u>

1. stew
2. flew
3. new

	Ramon	Kevin
Where they live	Dominican Republic	Maine, U.S.A.
What they do	Catcher on baseball team Going to party at aunt's house	Pitcher on baseball team Going on a picnic and to see fireworks
What they eat	Chicken stew with plantains, chicken, vegetables, sausage, and chicken feet	Chicken stew with chicken, noodles, and gravy

Page 88
1. The boys were hungry. OR The boys wanted a snack.
2. Grandmother was going to her computer class.
3. She said they could fix sandwiches.
4. Billy Joe ate peanut butter, honey, and banana.
5. Davy ate peanut butter and strawberry jam.
6. They drank milk.
7. Davy washed dishes. Billy Joe put things away.
8. Answers will vary, but could include:
   She didn't want their parents to worry.
   The boys had been at her house long enough.
   It was getting late.

Page 89
3
6
1
7
5
2
4

2   3   1

Page 90
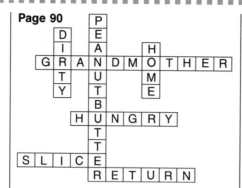

1. could eat an elephant
2. the roof of the mouth
3. scoot now

go away now
top part of the inside of the mouth
very, very hungry

Page 91
✗ thank
✗ with
(there)

(they)
✗ three
(then)

(them)
✗ think
✗ teeth

1. three
2. They
3. there
4. Thank
5. teeth
6. with
7. think

Page 94
1. The fruit you buy is grown in an orchard.
2. Blossoms change into fruit.
3. The fruit is picked at harvest time.
4. It gets ripe on the way to the supermarket.
5. Answers will vary.

Page 95
Pictures should include:
fruit growing on the tree
fruit being picked
Answers will vary, but could include:
apple pie, apple jelly, child eating apple, apples for sale

Page 96
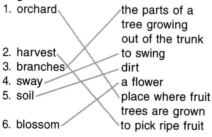

1. orchard
2. harvest
3. branches
4. sway
5. soil
6. blossom

the parts of a tree growing out of the trunk
to swing
dirt
a flower
place where fruit trees are grown
to pick ripe fruit

Sentences will vary.

Page 97
1. i	6. o	11. a
2. e	7. a	12. o
3. i	8. u	13. a
4. i	9. e	14. u
5. e	10. i	

1. red
2. eat
3. climb

Answers will vary, but could include:
1. book, cook, hook, look, shook
2. ball, call, fall, mall, wall
3. gown, town, clown, brown, frown
4. meet, beet, feet, tweet

Page 98

Answers will vary.

Page 100
1. It was built in an oak tree in the backyard.
2. lumber
   saw
   toolbox
   paint and brushes
   nails
   ladder
3. lumber—for the floor, walls, roof
   saw—to cut lumber
   nails—to hold the lumber in place
   brushes—to paint the tree house
4. It took a weekend to build the tree house.
5. Mother said no because it was going to rain.
6. There was a tree with low branches in the backyard.

Page 101
First, Dad carried lumber.
Second, Mom carried a ladder.
Third, Uncle Mike carried a saw.
Fourth, Kate carried paint and brushes.
Last, Jake carried the toolbox and nails.

1. Jake
2. Kate and Jake
3. Mom
4. Kate

Page 102

lumber   saw   toolbox
nails   sleeping bag ladder

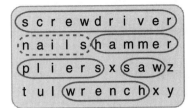

Page 103

Kate   paint   hay
clay   rake   nails

Page 106

1. Giant pandas are big with black-and-white fur.
2. Giant pandas live in bamboo forests in China.
3. (teeth) They help chew the bamboo.
   (hand and thumb) They help grab bamboo.
4. Newborn pandas are tiny. They don't have hair. Their eyes are closed.
5. They feed and protect their babies.
6. China set aside land so the pandas will have a safe place to live.

Page 107

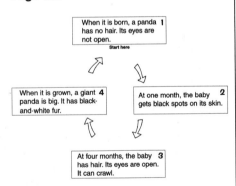

Page 108

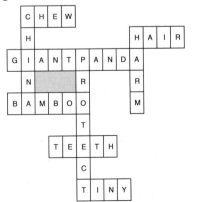

Page 109

1. g   5. g
2. j   6. j
3. j   7. g
4. g   8. j

1. grow
2. green grass
3. Grandmother, grape

Page 110

1. yes   6. yes
2. no   7. no
3. yes   8. no
4. no   9. yes
5. yes   10. yes

Pictures will vary, but must be some kind of bird.

Page 113

1. The hiker got the stone and the water from the farmer.
2. She went to the farmhouse for the onion.
3. She got the carrots from the garden.
4. He got the potatoes from the potato patch.
5. The hiker asked the farmer's family to come and have some soup.
6. The farmer wanted his wife to use the stone to make soup.
7. The hiker got the farmer's family to give him the vegetables to make soup.

Page 114

4
5
3
1
2

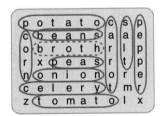

Page 115

1. message   5. scowl
2. folks   6. wife
3. hiker   7. loaf
4. wrong   8. autumn

1. stone/rock   4. stingy/selfish
2. merrily/happily 5. small/little
3. peeked/looked   6. dirt/soil

Page 116

1. old<u>er</u>   old<u>est</u>
2. young<u>er</u>   young<u>est</u>
3. tall<u>er</u>   tall<u>est</u>
4. fast<u>er</u>   fast<u>est</u>
5. cold<u>er</u>   cold<u>est</u>
6. soft<u>er</u>   soft<u>est</u>

1. older/younger
2. fastest
3. softer/older
4. tallest/oldest/youngest

1. 1   5. 3   9. 1
2. 3   6. 1   10. 3
3. 2   7. 2   11. 3
4. 2   8. 1   12. 2

Page 120

1. Beavers cut down trees, make dams, and make ponds.
2. a. see underwater
   b. steer in water
   c. dig and carry
   d. gnaw down trees
3. A beaver can stay underwater for 15 minutes.
4. Beavers push rocks on the logs to keep them from floating away.
5. A lodge looks like a large pile of sticks.
6. Answers will vary, but could include:
   They both cut wood into smaller pieces.
   They both build things out of wood.
   They both build places to live.

Page 121

3
5
1
4
2
6

Page 122

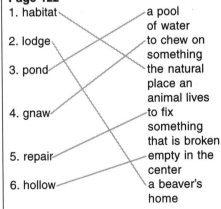

1. habitat
2. lodge
3. pond
4. gnaw
5. repair
6. hollow

a pool of water
to chew on something
the natural place an animal lives
to fix something that is broken
empty in the center
a beaver's home

More Read and Understand • Grade 2 • EMC 746

1. habitat
2. gnaw
3. lodge
4. hollow

Page 123
beaver   t<u>ee</u>th   w<u>e</u>
fift<u>ee</u>n   h<u>e</u>   str<u>ea</u>m

1. broad, flat
2. large orange
3. sharp

Page 124
bird   prairie dog
bees   spider

Page 126
1. Jamal heard a noise on the roof.
2. Jamal thought someone was trying to break into the house.
3. The noise was a raccoon dumping over the garbage can.
4. Dad shouted and flashed a light at them.
5. A raccoon can use its paws to take the lid off.
6. Dad was going to put hooks on the lid so the raccoons couldn't take it off.
7. Answers will vary, but should give reasons such as: Wild animals can hurt you. Wild animals might bite or scratch you.

Page 127
He heard a noise on the roof.
He ran to his parents' room.
There was a terrible noise in the backyard.
Dad took a flashlight to the backyard.
He scared off the raccoons.
Jamal helped clean up the mess.
"Tomorrow we will get hooks to keep the garbage can shut."

Page 128
1. c
2. b
3. c
4. c
5. a
6. b

Page 129
<u>food</u>
soon   room
boot   moon
school   noon

<u>look</u>
shook   stood
cook   wood
took   book

The order of the words will vary, but must include:
    fight, light, night, right, sight, tight

Sentences will vary.

Page 130
1. shouted   shouting
2. started   starting
3. knocked   knocking

1. pinned   pinning
2. trapped   trapping
3. begged   begging

1. shouting
2. knocked
3. trapped

Page 133
1. Carlos sat on the front step on a sunny afternoon.
2. a. cooing and crying
   b. laughing, singing, and jumping rope
   c. walking, talking, and buying ice cream
   d. shouting, joking, playing ball
   e. pushing strollers
   f. honking and driving
3. They stopped when they heard a siren.
4. The fire truck was on the way to a fire. OR The fire truck was going to an emergency.

1. they   5. he
2. it   6. we
3. she   7. it
4. he   8. they

Page 134
Carlos sat on the front step and watched people going by.
Suddenly everyone stopped.
A fire truck raced by.
The city sounds began again.

Picture should show firemen putting out a fire OR tending to another emergency.

Page 135

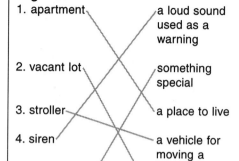

1. apartment
2. vacant lot
3. stroller
4. siren
5. cooing
6. treat

a loud sound used as a warning
something special
a place to live
a vehicle for moving a baby around
an empty area of land
a happy sound made by a baby

All but the following words should be circled:
car   what
ice cream   family
trucks

Page 136
slow<u>ly</u>   slow<u>er</u>
quiet<u>ly</u>   quiet<u>er</u>
soft<u>ly</u>   soft<u>er</u>
quick<u>ly</u>   quick<u>er</u>

1. sudden<u>ly</u>
2. slow<u>er</u>
3. old<u>er</u>
4. quiet<u>ly</u>
5. fast<u>er</u>

<u>Do</u>   <u>Did</u>
eat   drove
go   sat
sit   rode
laugh   went
drive   laughed
ride   ate

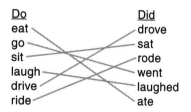